SPECTACULAR WINERIES
of California's Central Coast

A CAPTIVATING TOUR OF ESTABLISHED, ESTATE AND BOUTIQUE WINERIES

Published by

PANACHE
P A N A C H E   P A R T N E R S

Panache Partners, LLC
1424 Gables Court
Plano, TX 75075
469.246.6060
Fax: 469.246.6062
www.panache.com

Publishers: Brian G. Carabet and John A. Shand

Principal photographers: Peter Malinowski, Steve E. Miller, Maria
Villano and M.J. Wickham

Printed in Malaysia

Distributed by Independent Publishers Group
800.888.4741

PUBLISHER'S DATA

Spectacular Wineries of California's Central Coast

Library of Congress Control Number: 2009940501

ISBN 13: 978-1-933415-64-2
ISBN 10: 1-933415-64-9

First Printing 2010

10 9 8 7 6 5 4 3 2 1

Right: Conway Family Wines, page 30, *Photograph by Ian Shive*
Previous Page: Demetria Estate, page 158

Panache Partners, LLC, is dedicated to the restoration and
conservation of the environment. Our books are manufactured
with strict adherence to an environmental management system in
accordance with ISO 14001 standards, including the use of paper
from mills certified to derive their products from well-managed
forests. We are committed to continued investigation of alternative
paper products and environmentally responsible manufacturing
processes to ensure the preservation of our fragile planet.

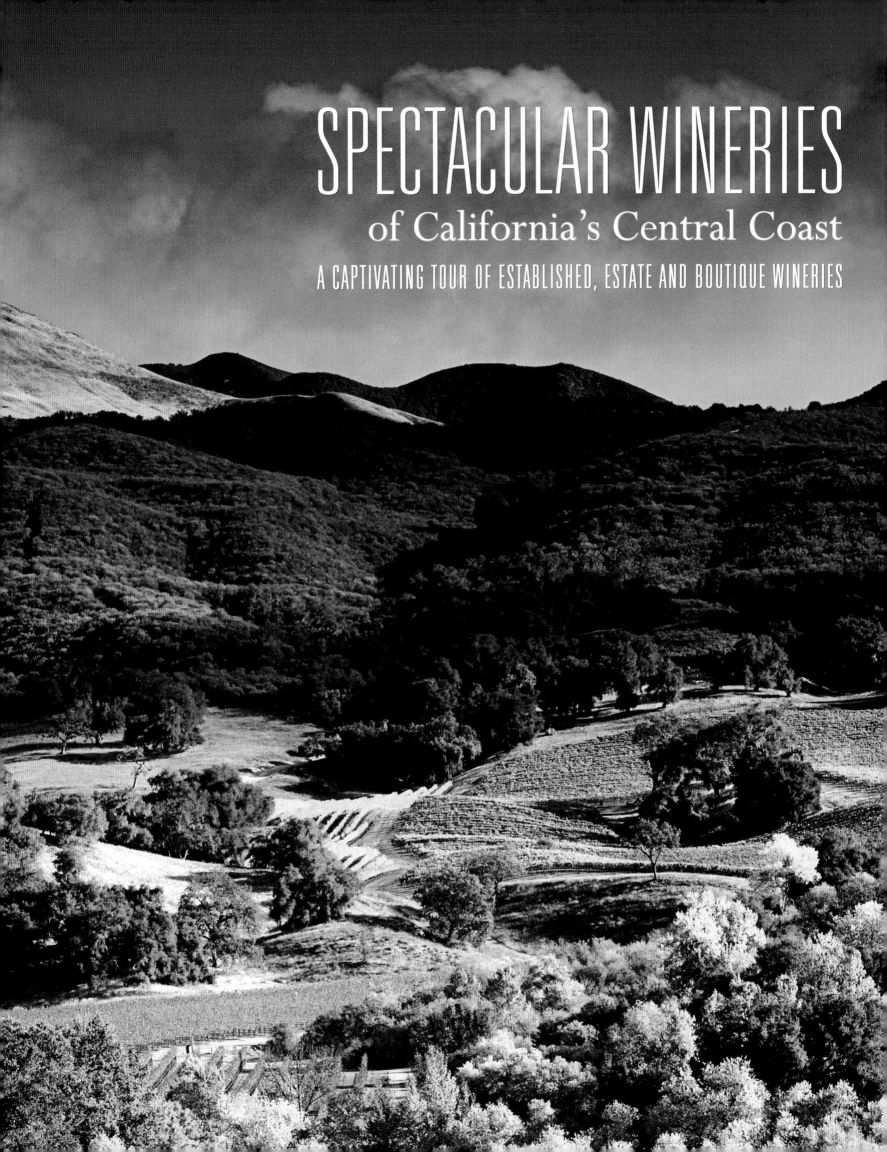

SPECTACULAR WINERIES
of California's Central Coast
A CAPTIVATING TOUR OF ESTABLISHED, ESTATE AND BOUTIQUE WINERIES

Paraíso Vineyards, page 140

Treana Winery and Hope Family Wines, page 110

You don't know it until you see it. You can't feel it until you've stood upon a rock formation above the vast Pacific and dared the wind and fog to blow you down, or experienced the intense desert-like heat of eastern Paso Robles. You can't know the wonders of this place even by tasting its array of magnificent wines. You have to be here, walking California's Central Coast vineyards, smelling the crisp ocean air, to know of its grandeur. For it is not a single place, convenient though its name may be. It is a broad collection of glorious places unique in the wine kingdom. People don't usually start their wine journey here, where wines have long lived in the shadow of more iconic places to the north—but the savvy sommelier, as well as the wine consumer, warms to the incredible expressions of vibrant fruit and flavor here. This volume triumphantly captures the spirit of visionary proprietors and vintners throughout the exceptional Central Coast winemaking region, which has rightfully earned its status in the world of wine.

Few places on earth offer greater diversity of soil, climate, and agriculture than the long and winding coastline from Santa Cruz down through Santa Barbara. Its broken volcanic formations open to numerous series of sedimentary soils and feature fine grape growing at elevations from sea level to over 2,000 feet. Its history as a wine producing region began with the 18th-century missionary migration up the coast, with the historic Franciscan worship of nature and its sacred products. It continued through the 19th century with early plantings of zinfandel and other European varieties, faltered with the painful hiccup of Prohibition, dozed into the middle of the 20th century as a bulk producer, and finally, in the 1960s and '70s, blossomed through the Herculean efforts of individuals who believed in quality wines.

Each distinctive sub-region has had its heroic pioneers—in the Santa Lucia Range and Santa Barbara County, pinot noir and chardonnay; in Santa Cruz, Paso Robles, Arroyo Grande Valley and Santa Ynez Valley,

syrah, viognier and other Rhône varieties; in Paso Robles, the Santa Cruz Mountains and Carmel Valley, the king of classic Bordeaux varieties, cabernet sauvignon. Yes, each of the wines derived from these varietals is inspired by an Old World model; and each is uniquely expressive of its New World style. Aside from France's classical inspiration, there have been whispers of winemaking influences from Germany, Italy, Spain and Portugal. American wine knows no limits when it comes to flattering its forebears.

Now we are seeing specialization really hone in on certain Central Coast AVAs. We understand the terroir and the water availability better than ever. Many producers are learning to do more with less—to cultivate sustainably, organically, and even biodynamically. Their respect for the place and its future is boundless.

Each and every vineyard and winery in California's Central Coast is worth a visit, and all have wine available through many avenues: wine clubs, regional and national retailers, and fine restaurants here and abroad. Seek them for great flavor and a reminder of the great land that produced them. Your palate will be rewarded!

—Joseph Spellman, MS

Chairman Emeritus, Court of Master Sommeliers, American Chapter

Sarah's Vineyard, page 184

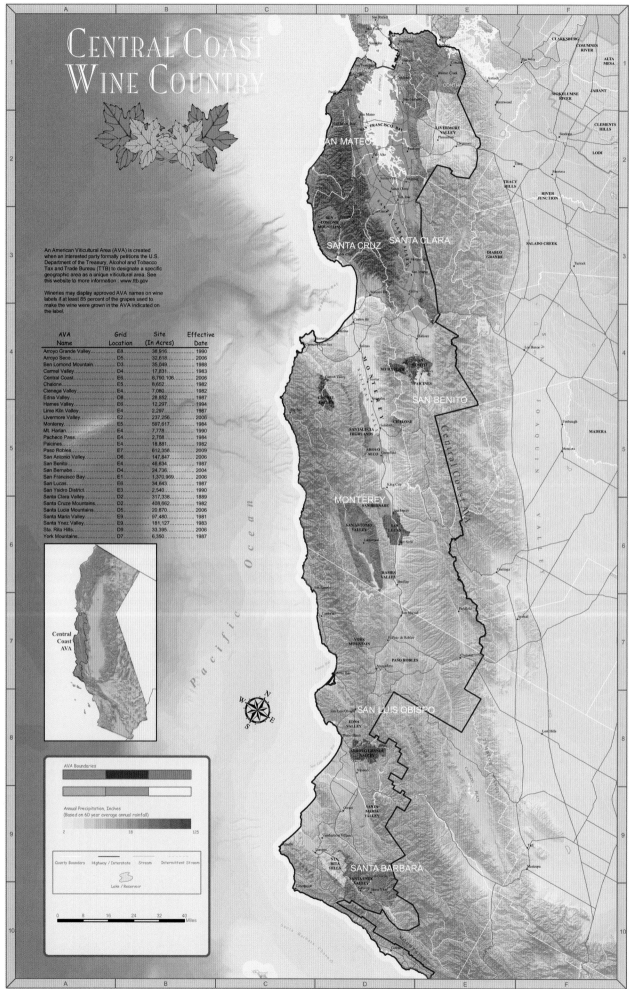

Central Coast Wine Country

An American Viticultural Area (AVA) is created when an interested party formally petitions the U.S. Department of the Treasury, Alcohol and Tobacco Tax and Trade Bureau (TTB) to designate a specific geographic area as a unique viticultural area. See this website to more information : www.ttb.gov

Wineries may display approved AVA names on wine labels if at least 85 percent of the grapes used to make the wine were grown in the AVA indicated on the label.

AVA Name	Grid Location	Site (In Acres)	Effective Date
Arroyo Grande Valley	E8	38,916	1990
Arroyo Seco	D5	32,818	2006
Ben Lomond Mountain	D3	35,049	1988
Carmel Valley	D4	17,831	1983
Central Coast	E6	6,790,106	2006
Chalone	E5	8,652	1982
Cienega Valley	E4	7,080	1982
Edna Valley	D8	28,852	1987
Hames Valley	E6	12,297	1994
Lime Kiln Valley	E4	2,297	1987
Livermore Valley	E2	237,256	2006
Monterey	E5	597,617	1984
Mt. Harlan	E4	7,778	1990
Pacheco Pass	E4	2,708	1984
Paicines	E4	18,881	1982
Paso Robles	E7	612,358	2009
San Antonio Valley	D6	147,847	2006
San Benito	E4	46,634	1987
San Bernabe	D4	24,736	2004
San Francisco Bay	E1	1,370,969	2006
San Lucas	E6	34,643	1987
San Ysidro District	E3	2,540	1990
Santa Clara Valley	D2	317,338	1889
Santa Cruz Mountains	D2	408,662	1982
Santa Lucia Mountains	D5	20,870	2006
Santa Maria Valley	E9	97,480	1981
Santa Ynez Valley	E9	181,127	1983
Sta. Rita Hills	D9	33,395	2006
York Mountains	D7	6,350	1987

Central Coast AVA

AVA Boundaries

Annual Precipitation, Inches
(Based on 60 year average annual rainfall)

2   18   125

County Boundary   Highway / Interstate   Stream   Intermittent Stream

Lake / Reservoir

0   8   16   24   32   40 Miles

Introduction

The saying "life is a journey, not a destination" may be cliché, but in the case of California's Central Coast and its evolution over time, pioneering winemakers and passionate dreamers have proven this tenet true. More than 200 years ago, Franciscan monks and early agricultural settlers brought the first European vine cuttings to the region—remnants of this historic era are still visible. Today the Central Coast AVA runs 250 miles from south of San Francisco down through Santa Barbara County, with hundreds of wineries producing grapes and award-winning vintages.

The Central Coast has expanded and matured into a well-known, world-class wine region. The 1990s saw a big influx of wineries and growth is steady, as more and more adventuresome winemakers make their way to the hallowed "ocean bed" ground of the Central Coast. With the region's proximity to the Pacific Ocean, microclimates play a big role in cool temperatures, dense fog and breezes allowing for longer growing seasons. The Central Coast is simply a winemaker's paradise.

Through this publishing experience I've gained an even fonder appreciation for the people, places and wines of the Central Coast. I've enjoyed the fervent support of the wineries, their communities and wine associations, especially the Paso Robles Wine Country Alliance and Monterey County Vintners and Growers Association. Not only did they welcome me with open arms when I moved to San Luis Obispo County a few years ago, they opened my eyes to the wonders of this rich region.

The unique flavor of the Central Coast is something you must experience for yourself. It's a place where winery founders and expert winemakers mingle with visitors like old family and friends. Their genuine passion for the land and the fruits of their labors is clear. My sincere gratitude goes out to each winery proprietor, the creative winemakers and everyone who has helped to make this beautiful book so special. Ciao!

—Carla Bowers
Regional Publisher

Photograph by Peter Bowers

Table of Contents

San Luis Obispo County

Monterey County

"Growing grapes in the area was a stretch of imagination when I planted the first vineyard in the Santa Rita Hills almost 40 years ago. Reality has overcome imagination as the appellation is now recognized for producing world-class wines."

—Richard Sanford, Alma Rosa Winery & Vineyards

"For all of us who have put down winegrowing roots here on the Central Coast, and dedicated ourselves to realizing its potential for viticultural greatness, there is profound satisfaction in seeing it take its rightful place as one of the world's great wine regions."

—Cynthia Lohr, J. Lohr Vineyards & Wines

"You cannot come to Paso Robles without experiencing one of the greatest pleasures in life, a beautiful glass of wine combined with a great experience. The wines are great, the country is beautiful and the folks are like none you've ever met."

—Doug Beckett, Peachy Canyon Winery

Soquel Vineyards, page 198

Adelaida Cellars, page 22

Bien Nacido Vineyards, page 206

Sycamore Creek Vineyards & Winery, page 190

Rhône Rangers, page 212

Tablas Creek Vineyard, page 98

Kenneth Volk Vineyards, page 162

Vina Robles Winery, page 122

Veris Cellars, page 116

Chalone Vineyard, page 130

Maloy O'Neill Vineyards, page 64

Sculpterra Winery & Sculpture Garden, page 82

Conway Family Wines, page 90

Sylvester Vineyards & Winery, page 94

"The Central Coast is an enchanting place for wine lovers and a winemaker's paradise. One can taste the very essence of terroir in the wines, from the minerality of the calcareous soils of Paso Robles to the great natural acidity of the coastal microclimates. Our family has planted its flag here to stay and will remain for many generations to come."

—Daniel and Georges Daou, Daou Vineyards

"I love the Central Coast grape-growing area. There are multiple macro and microclimates all along the way, with immense variations of climate, soil types and terrain, from flat alluvial soils on broad fertile valleys to rugged mountaintop vineyards with vineyards planted as high at 2,500 feet above sea level. Premium fruit comes from the Central Coast, thus premium wines are naturally born."

—Josh Jensen, Calera Wine Company

"At Hahn Winery we have always focused on the significance of the Central Coast which includes our vineyards in Monterey and the Santa Lucia Highlands. From the beginning, we were inspired by the rugged beauty and natural abundance of the region. The result is that our wines are a reflection of the diversity of California's expansive Central Coast."

—Nicolaus Hahn, Hahn Family Wines

"Growing grapes and making wine is such a unique lifestyle, it's 24 hours a day, 7 days a week. Do I love it? Unquestionably. I've never done anything else in my life. I'd say that Paso Robles, and the entire Central Coast, has a special personality that you have to experience for yourself."

—Gary Eberle, Eberle Winery

Talbott Vineyards, page 144

Treana Winery and Hope Family Wines, page 110

David Bruce Winery, page 194

Bien Nacido Vineyards, page 206

Justin Vineyards & Winery, page 58

Anne Thull Fine Art Designs, page 204

Steinbeck Vineyards & Winery, page 218

Tablas Creek Vineyard, page 98

Kenneth Volk Vineyards, page 162

Demetria Estate, page 158

Conway Family Wines, page 30

Kenneth Volk Vineyards, page 162

"The Central Coast wine country is a broad and diverse winemaking region providing unique soils and microclimates that allow each winemaker to create a true signature style. This makes for brand diversity within the region and creativity on the part of each winemaker. We have our own estate vineyards to work with but also utilize long-term growers from around our area to allow depth and complexity from different vineyard sites."

—Justin and Deborah Baldwin, Justin Vineyards & Winery

"A great wine is one with wonderful varietal characteristics and the ability to hold those characteristics for a long period of time. Those wonderful characteristics are a noble robe, that velvety texture and fruit-forwardness."

—David Bruce, David Bruce Winery

Peachy Canyon Winery, page 68

Windward Vineyard, page 124

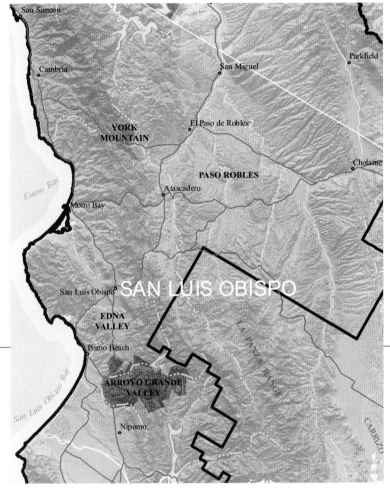

San Luis Obispo

County

Map provided by www.vestra.com

Adelaida Cellars

Paso Robles

I t all began as a neighborly business relationship. In 1991, the Van Steenwyk family partnered with John Munch—who lived just down Adelaida Road—to build a winery on their Hilltop Ranch. John had established the label 10 years earlier when he moved to California's Central Coast in search of the perfect growing conditions. The Van Steenwyks had arrived somewhat earlier and invested in a successful walnut-producing ranch known as the Hilltop. After the family's farm advisor told them they had ideal conditions for growing grapes as well, the Munches and Van Steenwyks joined forces to create the present-day Adelaida Cellars; its first vineyards were planted that same year. In 1999, John moved down Adelaida Road again to found his own winery.

Just a century earlier, the Adelaida farming community was known for its abundant crops of fruit, nuts, grain and hay and raising livestock. But it became apparent that this region was a hidden geological gem with great potential for producing premium winegrapes to craft distinctive varietals and blends. The promising area had always been renowned for its aesthetic beauty with mountains, valleys, streams and oak trees. Its calcareous soils and cool microclimates have since proven to be perfect for growing grapes worthy of fine winemaking.

Many of Adelaida Cellars' wines currently originate from two prolific estate vineyards: Viking Estate Vineyard and the historic HMR Estate Vineyard, formerly Hoffman Mountain Ranch, acquired by the Van Steenwyks in 1994. The 400-acre site on Adelaida Road is home to several varieties including the venerable pinot noir vineyard developed in 1964 by Dr. Stanley Hoffman with legendary winemaker André Tchelistcheff's vision at its heart. Other estate vineyards producing for Adelaida Cellars are Bobcat Crossing, Anna's and Michael's Vineyards—each named for a family of bobcats, a special grandmother, and one close friend.

Top Left: Bottles of HMR Estate Pinot Noir beckon enophiles to California's Central Coast, and especially the Paso Robles appellation.
Photograph by Maria Villano

Bottom Left: A cabernet sauvignon cluster in HMR Estate Vineyard slowly ripens in late August.
Photograph by JAG Public Relations

Facing Page: HMR Estate Vineyard offers challenging slopes and venerable vines originally planted in 1964.
Photograph by Maria Villano

From these unique estate vineyards, winemaker Terry Culton transforms vineyard harvests into award-winning single varietal pinot noir, cabernet sauvignon, chardonnay and popular zinfandel as well as innovative Rhône Valley-inspired blends of counoise, mourvèdre, syrah, viognier and roussanne produced under the Reserve, Adelaida and Schoolhouse labels. With dedicated years of experience working alongside veteran vintners Josh Jensen of Calera and pioneering Paso Robles winemaker Kenneth Volk, Terry has brought his vast knowledge and excitement to the winemaking process at Adelaida.

"Our wines are truly vineyard-driven," says Elizabeth Van Steenwyk. Terry agrees that his craft embraces this same honest philosophy: "The wine is the pure essence of our vineyards." Tasting the results of his labors, there is only one conclusion—Adelaida wines are an undeniable part of Paso Robles' magic. The vintner's portfolio is now known for garnering critical acclaim and the attention of the national wine community, as well as expressing the truest reflection of the area's limestone soils.

The historical 1800s schoolhouse in the Adelaida district was the winery's inspiration for the Schoolhouse label, featuring vintage Recess Red, which has become a favorite of Adelaida fans. Sampling the portfolio of Adelaida wines is an enlightening experience for all visitors. Barrel tastings offer samples aged in French oak that impart hints of sweet earthiness. Sylvia, the storybook cat, mingles

Top Left: Custom doors at the main entrance were cut from the oak staves of a huge, recycled fermentation tank.

Bottom Left: A light and airy tasting room welcomes visitors seven days a week.

Facing Page: Acknowledging the region's limestone bedrock, a stone masonry wall marks the winery entrance on Adelaida Road.
Photographs by Maria Villano

with guests as they taste new releases in the tasting room or at one of the seasonal events. The owners have a passion for educating visitors, whether through Library Tasting Sundays with its two-hour course in wine appreciation, or at an Author Faire book signing with highly informed writers and wine experts on hand to share advice.

After more than 17 years, Adelaida Cellars has established a reputation for creating critically acclaimed wines with many of their varietals receiving Robert Parker's 90-plus reviews, while the well-tended estate vineyards continue to flourish in the Paso Robles appellation on the central coast of California.

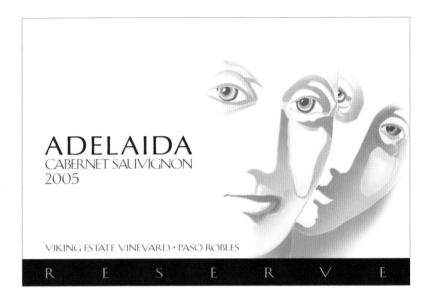

ADELAIDA
CABERNET SAUVIGNON
2005

VIKING ESTATE VINEYARD · PASO ROBLES

R E S E R V E

WINE & FARE

Adelaida Version White
(grenache, blanc, roussanne)

Pair with scallops, Asian curry dishes, fire-grilled vegetables or fresh mozzarella cheese.

Adelaida HMR Estate Pinot Noir

Pair with coq au vin, pheasant, game hens, Pacific salmon and wild mushrooms.

Adelaida Version Red
(mourvèdre, grenache, syrah, counoise, cinsault)

Pair with cassoulet, pork tenderloin, sheep's milk cheese, cured meats or prosciutto.

Adelaida Viking Estate Cabernet Sauvignon
(96% cabernet sauvignon, 4% cabernet franc)

Pair with grilled meats or venison, lamb or prime-aged beef.

Tastings
Open to the public daily, year-round

Baileyana and Tangent Wineries

San Luis Obispo

Founded upon rich historical roots, Baileyana Winery began when Catharine Niven planted a small three-acre vineyard in her front yard; her husband Jack had introduced winegrape planting to the pristine Edna Valley of San Luis Obispo County during the early 1970s. Pioneers in the newly discovered winemaking region of California's Central Coast, Catharine and Jack began a fulfilling journey and were later joined by sons John R. and James, who remain actively involved, along with grandsons Michael Blaney and John H. Niven. The enthusiastic third-generation team manages the day-to-day operations of the family-owned estate. Today the multigenerational entrepreneurs are internationally recognized as prominent vintners; the family has been dedicated to firmly establishing eight-mile-long Edna Valley as one of California's most important cool-climate winemaking regions.

A unique concept, Baileyana and Tangent Wineries coexist under one roof, each highly focused with its own identity offering distinctively different wine portfolios. Baileyana creates traditional, Old World-inspired estate wines derived from its estate Firepeak Vineyard grapes, producing handcrafted chardonnay, pinot noir and syrah. These classic varietals are oak-barrel aged imparting more traditional flavors. In sharp contrast, Tangent winery was an idea conceived in 2005 by John H. and Michael, designed to produce alternative white varietals from its estate Paragon Vineyard harvests. Tangent wines have zero oak influence, ensuring pure varietal character, and are bottled sans cork with a decidedly contemporary brand image. Tangent uses atypical varietals to create alternative whites such as the aromatic albariño, a grape native to northwestern Spain and grown in the Nivens' well-nurtured albariño vineyard, one of the largest in

Top Left: This view captures a prized block of Clone 115 pinot noir grown in Baileyana's Estate Firepeak Vineyard.
Photograph by Chris Leschinsky

Bottom Left: Burgundian born and trained winemaker Christian Roguenant brings his expertise and years of experience to every handcrafted bottle.
Photograph by Barry Goyette

Facing Page: Baileyana and Tangent's estate vineyards are nestled amidst the coastal hills of picturesque Edna Valley.
Photograph by Chris Leschinsky

the United States. Other Tangent varietals include the familiar sauvignon blanc from the estate's 35-year-old grapevines, as well as pinot gris, pinot blanc, riesling and viognier. Future harvests will yield the highly praised grüner veltliner of Austria's and Spain's treixadura and loureira, often blended with albariño. These premier quality Tangent alternative white wines are meant to be enjoyed young.

Seasoned winemaker Christian Roguenant is particularly passionate about his award-winning Baileyana chardonnay, pinot and syrah. Burgundian born, he has an affinity for the fine art of French winemaking and boasts more than two decades of experience working for leading Champagne houses. Christian earned his sophisticated winemaking education from the University of Dijon; he brings vast experience and creativity to Baileyana and Tangent. The winemaker has worked on five continents: Europe, Australia, South America, Asia and North America. His broad winemaking repertoire has been welcomed by the Nivens since he joined the family operation in 1998. The visionary winemaker was also instrumental in bringing to fruition the wineries' state-of-the-art production facility with its gracious architecture, especially geared to world-class pinot noir and syrah, which both demand delicate handling. Continually striving for winemaking perfection, Christian carefully hand selects ripened grapes to capture the essence of the vineyards, crafting outstanding traditional and alternative wines that consistently receive rave reviews.

Top Left: A restored jewel, the 100-year-old historic Independence Schoolhouse is home to the tasting room for Baileyana and Tangent wineries.
Photograph by J.P. Drape

Middle Left: Firepeak Vineyard's unique mix of volcanic soils and marine deposits epitomize the Central Coast's regional terroir.
Photograph by J.P. Drape

Bottom Left: The contemporary Tangent family of alternative white wines includes atypical varietals.
Photograph by Samson Pinto

Facing Page: The Baileyana Grand Firepeak Cuvee wines possess classic, Old World flavors.
Photograph by Samson Pinto

The property's historic Independence Schoolhouse dates back to 1909—this charming schoolhouse-turned-tasting room greets guests with Baileyana and Tangent wine samples. The Nivens restored the original one-room structure to reveal an updated version in 1998. Both their Paragon and Firepeak vineyards surround the tasting room that provides visitors with scenic veranda views ideal for sipping new releases from both wineries while imbibing friendly conversation. Distributed in seven countries, Baileyana and Tangent wines are within reach of those who want to experience award-winning tastes from the jewel of the Edna Valley with true California family heritage in every bottle.

WINE & FARE

Baileyana Grand Firepeak Cuvee Chardonnay
(100% chardonnay)

Pair with classic crab cakes or butter-poached lobster tail.

Baileyana Grand Firepeak Cuvee Pinot Noir
(100% pinot noir)

Pair with grilled salmon or roasted leg of lamb.

Tangent Sauvignon Blanc
(100% sauvignon blanc)

Pair with spicy chicken salad or grilled scallops.

Tangent Albariño
(100% albariño)

Pair with fresh oysters on the half shell or poached sea bass.

Tastings
Open to the public daily, year-round

Conway Family Wines

Arroyo Grande

I f a Central Coast terroir could talk, the Arroyo Grande Valley appellation would surely have something important to say. With its natural dramatic topography surrounded by ridgelines on three sides, a moderate climate, abundant wildlife and fossil soils, the Conway Family Wines vineyards and winery are proud to make their home on historical Rancho Arroyo Grande, the 1841 Spanish Land Grant encompassing 3,400 acres of grape-growing splendor. The exposed soils are remnants of an ancient seabed uplifted over millions of years, and the shell embossing on the estate label, Rancho Arroyo Grande, exemplifies their contribution to the wines.

After acquiring the ranch inclusive of vineyards, olive groves and equine center in 2007, Chris and Ann Conway collaborated with daughter Gillian and sons Gareth and Thomas to realize Conway Family Wines. The Conways have dedicated themselves to farming three estate vineyards planted on 230 acres that range from 400 to 1,000 feet in elevation on sprawling flatland and rolling terrain. The Zeferino, Coquina and Potrero Vineyards produce grape yields that are transformed into estate-derived Rancho Arroyo Grande wines featuring Rhône varietals and zinfandel; mourvèdre is fast becoming a rising star with 90-point ratings. The winery also extends its programs to feature highly acclaimed maritime-influenced vineyards throughout California's coastal appellations, particularly chardonnay and pinot noir under the DEEP SEA label.

Top Left: Rancho Arroyo Grande estate vineyards—totaling more than 200 acres—is planted with Rhône varietals including syrah, mourvèdre, grenache, counoise and viognier.

Middle Left: Feral peacocks and other native wildlife roam the sprawling hillsides, pastures and vineyards on the estate.

Bottom Left: Gareth, Gillian and Thomas Conway devote their energies to creating a family of interesting and appealing wines.

Facing Page: Estate Coquina Vineyard—named after the fossil-rich soils of the ranch—thrives on beautiful rolling hills.
Photographs by Ian Shive

Esteemed winemakers Andrew Adam and Jonathan Medard specialize in crafting Conway's selection of wines; the winery's production focuses on creative blends and single varietals, mainly syrah, grenache, mourvèdre, chardonnay and zinfandel. The Conway family's winemaking philosophy is to protect the integrity of the grapes, bringing the fruit's intrinsic qualities to full expression in the wine. Showcasing the diversity of regions, from the ranch estate to the maritime appellations, throughout California, and capturing the specific terroir of each varietal in the final wines, has become the Conway Family Wines signature.

Top Left: Estate Zeferino Vineyard was named in honor of Zeferino Carlon, the original grantee of Rancho Arroyo Grande.

Middle Left: Evolved from ancient sea beds, the soils of Rancho Arroyo Grande abound with fossilized shells; rich mineral content supports wines of complexity and mystery.

Bottom Left: Framed by the peaks of the Los Padres, the active ranch provides a home for horses, bison and cattle.

Facing Page: The Rancho Arroyo Grande label was inspired by fossilized scallops found in the soils of the estate vineyards.
Photographs by Ian Shive

Creating intriguing wines born from the historically rich land and building a legacy to last for future generations is double inspiration for the Conways. Plans are underway for their new hospitality center and innovative winery facility designed to be environmentally efficient with gravity-flow technology, temperature controls through sustainable straw bale construction and architecture designed to fit seamlessly into its sublime surroundings, thus preserving the poetic beauty of Rancho Arroyo Grande.

Wine & Fare

DEEP SEA Chardonnay

Pair with oysters grilled over French oak staves with fennel and wild herbs drizzled with Rancho Arroyo Grande Estate olive oil.

Rancho Arroyo Grande Mourvèdre

Pair with Asian-style short ribs with sweet and spicy chili sauce.

Rancho Arroyo Grande Zinfandel

Pair with traditional Mexican chocolate cake made with cocoa powder and a hint of cinnamon.

DEEP SEA Red

Pair with sea salt-encrusted rack of lamb with rosemary and balsamic marinade.

Tastings
Open by appointment only, year-round

Daou Vineyards

Paso Robles

The Daou brothers abide by the French philosophy of joie de vivre in all that they do: a joy of witty conversation, a joy of eating and a joy of winemaking. Raised in France, Daniel and Georges were introduced to good wine at an early age by their father, who served every meal with a glass of wine. Not only did the family have a love of fine wine, they also had a strong agricultural heritage, having been involved in olive oil production. The brothers often reminisced about their olive farm and dreamed of re-creating the same rewarding lifestyle for themselves someday.

Daniel and Georges came to the United States in the '80s, pursuing college degrees in engineering at the University of California San Diego, which brought them even closer to their destiny. After founding a technology company and growing it to a successful IPO in 1997, the young entrepreneurs retired and began to recapture their childhood dream. Exploring wine country in Napa Valley, Sonoma County and as far away as Argentina, they searched for the perfect terroir. But none compared to their fortuitous discovery: 100 acres of coveted land on the west side of Paso Robles in the Adelaida region, with its calcareous, high-percentage limestone soils, maritime climate and remarkable potential for growing Bordeaux-style varietals. This unique winemaking region with its remarkable limestone deposits was discovered by André Tchelistcheff in the 1970s and was part of the original Hoffman Mountain Ranch winery that has produced world-class wines made in the French tradition. Daniel's vision was to produce a cabernet-focused Bordeaux-style blend that would rival the world's best, and these limestone-rich soils spelled success.

Top Left: Captured in soft morning light, the Daou Vineyards' wrought-iron gate marks the land.
Photograph by Peter Malinowski

Middle Left: Brothers Georges and Daniel celebrate their debut 2006 release: Daou Cabernet Sauvignon.
Photograph by Peter Malinowski

Bottom Left: Nutrient-rich soils on Daou Vineyards include Ayar, Balcom, Linne Calodo and Nacimiento.
Photograph by Bruce Woodworth

Facing Page: Spectacular sunrises grace the estate; the vista is from atop Daou Mountain in the Adelaida district of Paso Robles.
Photograph by Peter Malinowski

The creative Daou brothers realized their joint vision by acquiring this special terroir with its renowned reputation. Today, "Live the dream, come to Paso" is the dynamic duo's daily mantra.

The Daou Vineyards estate is planted with select varietals including cabernet sauvignon, cabernet franc, petit verdot, syrah, merlot and zinfandel. Grapevines thrive on the fossil-rich soil at 2,233 feet above sea level; the mountain estate is so high you can almost touch the clouds. Guests have exuberantly expressed the feeling of being on "Cloud 9" when the morning fog envelops the vineyards. The combination of diverse soils, a rare microclimate and an incredibly high elevation holds the secret to fruit perfection, while southeast-southwest sun exposures allow grapes to evenly ripen. "Altitude becomes your

attitude…and high altitude vineyards simply produce great wines," says Georges. The vigneron brothers' high-energy personalities and upbeat sense of humor are as vivacious as the awe-inspiring mountain region they cultivate.

Above: The Daou family often gathers at the vineyard to enjoy a picnic and the wonderful view.
Photograph by Peter Malinowski

Right: Georges and Melissa relax with Daou winery dogs Ruppi and Grussie.
Photograph by Peter Malinowski

Facing Page Top: An awe-inspiring panoramic view clearly shows the dramatic high altitude and steepness of vineyard slopes.
Photograph by Peter Bowers

Facing Page Bottom: The entrance to Daou Vineyards offers a breathtaking view overlooking vineyard blocks 6 and 7.
Photograph by Peter Malinowski

On Daou Mountain plantings are dense; up to 2,333 vines per acre produce six to eight clusters of grapes, making at most a single bottle of wine per vine. The low-yield crops symbolize the brothers' focus on quality fruit versus quantity. Dedicated growers and vintners, their commitment to organic farming practices is paramount. Naturally nurtured, handpicked, hand-sorted grapes are transformed into elegant handcrafted red wines aged for up to 22 months in French oak barrels. New vintages are expected to be born from the estate's first harvest with an exceptional line of Daou wine releases to follow—the envisioned wine is a proprietary Bordeaux-style blend incorporating cabernet sauvignon, cabernet franc, merlot and petit verdot. Winemaker Daniel—mentored by the illustrious enologist Delphine Barboux-Laurent from Château Lascombes in Margaux—will also bottle small amounts of zinfandel and

a couture cabernet-syrah blend. Daniel's discerning palate and driving passion are truly reflected in every drop of Daou Vineyards wine.

Visitors enter the wrought-iron gated vineyards to enjoy the delicious Daou experience in the estate's ultra-hip tasting room, and small groups can arrange guided ATV tours through the vineyards for a true farmer's perspective. As guests step onto the wide open deck for a taste of fine wine

Above: Daou Vineyards is situated 2,200 feet above sea level. A rare and beautiful sight, the vineyards were blanketed with snow in winter 2008, underscoring their high elevation.
Photograph by James Hendon

Facing Page: Visitors can taste fine vintages while experiencing what it means to "Live the dream, come to Paso."
Photograph by Peter Malinowski

and the good life, they enjoy a view that transports them to another world. Wise oak trees dot the brothers' ancient property, whispering local legends of people gathered there making bootlegged alcohol a century ago. Times have changed. Romance is in the breeze at Daou Vineyards. "From vine to wine" is the song the winds sing, while a rare Spanish monastery bell circa 1740 rings out in celebration as each complex wine emerges, seducing guests to sip, smell the roses and experience the magic of Paso Robles.

WINE & FARE

Daou Cabernet Sauvignon

Pair with rib eye steak with a red wine demi-glace accompanied by exotic mushrooms and field greens.

Daou Celestus Blend

Pair with gigot d'agneau (roasted leg of lamb) with rosemary or thyme pan sauce served with potatoes, green beans and eggplant timbale.

Daou Zinfandel

Pair with traditional Italian pasta dishes such as tagliatelle al ragù.

Tastings

Open by appointment only

Eberle Winery

Paso Robles

A newly acquired taste for fine wine and an intuitive spark transported Gary Eberle from working on his doctorate in genetics at Charity Hospital in New Orleans to Paso Robles, eager to explore the world of winemaking. It was a group of tenured professors who inspired Gary. They would invite the doctoral student over for stimulating intellectual conversation, dinner and a variety of wines in the course of an evening, which introduced Gary to wines savored by more sophisticated drinkers.

Captivated by good wine and winemaking methods, he headed for UC Davis to study fermentation science with his published genetics papers and patents in hand. His newfound passion quickly transformed into reality. After earning his degree in the viticulture program, Gary was instrumental in co-founding the Paso Robles appellation based on thorough study of the area's geology and weather patterns. "In 1973 we were high on the possibilities of Paso Robles," Gary shares. With unbridled enthusiasm and visionary ideas, he and a friend drew up the original boundaries for one of California's first designated grape-growing regions, putting the Paso Robles AVA on the world winemaking map.

It has been 30 years since Gary started Eberle Winery. His German family name of Eberle means "little boar," which instantly became the brand mascot—an Italian artist's cast bronze wild boar sculpture identifies the entrance to the landmark winery. The namesake winery label is embossed with its famous wild boar logo, now etched in the minds of a loyal following. Producing nearly 30,000 cases of estate wines annually, the picturesque property includes 65 acres with 17,000 feet of wine cave tunnels, an impressive 40-acre estate vineyard and a cozy wine-tasting room. First plantings took root in 1974 on this

Top Left: Oak barrels filled with handcrafted Port age to perfection in the Eberle wine caves.

Bottom Left: Stylized stained glass grapevine designs on the winery doors greet visitors.

Facing Page: Rustic niches in the Eberle wine caves spotlight popular library wines.
Photographs by Steve E. Miller

renowned vineyard known for its prolific estate-grown cabernet sauvignon, chardonnay and muscat canelli. Many wineries have sprung up around Gary's original Paso Robles estate, starting with clones derived from his precious syrah vines known for outstanding fruit yields.

Paso Robles' vintners fondly refer to Gary's winery as "Eberle U" based on his dedicated mentoring of viticulture students over the years and his successful non-profit scholarship foundation. The family-owned winery owes recent success to resident winemaker Ben Mayo, who has developed a distinguished collection of award-winning Eberle wines earning numerous gold medals and industry recognition throughout California, the United States and Europe. From the extraordinary reserve cabernet to California's highest-honored viognier, Eberle's winemaking philosophy is pure and simple: The wine in the bottle should taste like the grape on the vine. Gently culled, hand-harvested grapes produce elegant, well-balanced varietals that capture the essence of the fruit. Ranked in size as the 26th largest of 171 area wineries, the small family-owned winery is proud of its winecrafting heritage and longstanding reputation.

Top Left: The Eberle Wild Boar Room is an elegant setting for monthly guest chef dinners as well as special events.

Bottom Left: Eberle's flagship wines include estate cabernet sauvignon and chardonnay with labels featuring the "little boar."

Facing Page: All Eberle's wines mature in authentic oak barrels stacked in naturally cool Eberle wine caves.
Photographs by Steve E. Miller

Gary and his wife Marcy, the winery's marketing and public relations director, are both avid wine educators. The couple insists that each guest experience an exclusive winery tour complete with regional vintners' secrets and private barrel tastings. The winery's Wild Boar Room offers a coveted dining experience. The owners have garnered a reputation for hosting monthly events with world-renowned chefs offering wine and food pairings that showcase selections from their 13 delicious varietals matched with perfect accompaniments. And just like Eberle's elegant yet approachable wines, the family's two standard poodles, Cabernet and Roussanne, delight visitors with their irresistible character and friendly nature.

PASO ROBLES

CABERNET SAUVIGNON
ESTATE BOTTLED

WINE & FARE

Eberle Estate Cabernet Sauvignon
(100% cabernet sauvignon)

Pair with filet mignon, leg of lamb or Gary's famous barbecue ribs.

Eberle Barbera
(100% barbera)

Pair with classic dishes such as short ribs, venison, rack of lamb, meat lasagne or duck served with a rich sauce.

Eberle "Mill Road" Viognier

Pair with Pan-Pacific cuisine, from spicy Thai noodles to tuna tartar or shellfish such as baked lobster tail and fresh raw oysters.

Eberle Estate Muscat Canelli

Pair with classic desserts including cheesecake, crème brûlée and almond biscotti, or with an array of soft cheeses, dried fruit and roasted nuts.

Tastings
Open to the public daily, year-round

Edna Valley Vineyard

San Luis Obispo

One of California's best kept secrets, Edna Valley Vineyard is a landmark winery that was founded in 1973 by pioneer vintner John Niven; he established an enterprise that was clearly ahead of its time, as the Central Coast first revealed its winemaking prowess on the world stage in Paris 1976. Nestled a mere five miles from the Pacific Ocean in the heart of the fruitful Edna Valley AVA, Edna Valley Vineyard is known for its lush hillsides with panoramic vineyard views, making it a veritable paradise for viticulturists and visitors. The region is said to possess the intoxicating air of romance that Napa Valley had 30 years ago.

Award-winning wines that exhibit distinct varietal flavor, intense richness and perfect balance are the result of the uniquely long and temperate growing season, ideal soil conditions and mountainous terrain that captures cool marine air directly over Edna Valley Vineyard. More than 25 million years ago, the land was enriched by layers of marine sediment—rich clay, seashells and beach sand—which formed a fertile, wide-mouthed funnel between ocean and land. A chain of 14 eroding volcanic cones lies between Morro Bay and Edna Valley Vineyard, further enhancing the quality of the land.

Classic Burgundian techniques are at the core of Edna Valley Vineyard's minimalist approach to winemaking. Grapes are handled gently, and wine is fermented and aged in imported French oak barrels with little intervention along the way. Edna Valley Vineyard is best known for producing world-class chardonnays and pinot noirs while syrah and

Top Left: The winery's welcoming patio invites guests to enjoy the view of the garden and vineyards.
Photograph by Alan Campbell

Bottom Left: Edna Valley Vineyard has one of the longest and coolest growing seasons in California with grapes harvested through late October.
Photograph by Alan Campbell

Facing Page: Looking out from the tasting room, Islay Peak rises above the vineyards. The surrounding hills and mountains capture marine air flowing in from Morro Bay, creating climatic conditions unique to Edna Valley.
Photograph by Peter Malinowski

sauvignon blanc are its rising stars. Cabernet and merlot, sourced from consistently top-rated Paso Robles, are the newest additions to the Edna Valley Vineyard family.

Edna Valley Vineyard represents a unique partnership between Diageo Chateau & Estate Wines and the Niven family, who owns Paragon Vineyard. Harry Hansen and Josh Baker partner as the esteemed winemaking team; both have vast experience handcrafting chardonnay and pinot noir. Acclaimed for their creativity, clonal research and evaluation, they have brought Edna Valley Vineyard into the limelight by blending science and art.

The art of growing grapes has undergone a revolution since 1973, with the introduction of new clones, new rootstocks and a range of new cultivation techniques. Harry and Josh worked alongside the Niven family to incorporate many of these viticultural advances into the new vineyard blocks when Paragon Vineyard replanted 65 acres of pinot noir in the 1990s. The replanted blocks nurture six different pinot noir clones selected for their distinctive character and proven ability to perform in a cool climate. Beginning with the 2000 vintage, these newly rooted grapevines have transformed the vineyard's pinot noir from excellent to internationally noteworthy.

Top Left: The barrel room is a special setting for club members to sip and savor Edna Valley Vineyard signature wines.
Photograph by Alan Campbell

Bottom Left: Edna Valley Vineyard is one of the few wineries in San Luis Obispo to host spectacular weddings that make a lasting impression.
Photograph by Belle Castle Photography

Facing Page: Focusing on estate-grown chardonnay, the veteran growers have a strong commitment to producing pinot noir, syrah, sauvignon blanc, merlot and cabernet sauvignon using new varietal clones.
Photograph by Geoff Nilsen

Sophisticated winemaking requires an eye on the future, and Edna Valley Vineyard employs the latest technology coupled with traditional artisan winemaking techniques so that every bottle captures the delicious and delicate fruit of the vines derived from Edna Valley's fertile terroir. The Jack Niven Hospitality Center pays homage to the winery founder and welcomes guests to taste the latest releases reflecting decades of winemaking heritage. Destination weddings, outdoor receptions, meetings and special events often grace the vineyard—its inspiring landscape makes the perfect backdrop for so many social occasions. Fabulous scenery and a relaxed ambience aside, it is Edna Valley Vineyard's award-winning wines that have guests falling in love.

EDNA VALLEY
VINEYARD ®

WINE & FARE

Edna Valley Vineyard Chardonnay
(100% chardonnay)
Pair with tarragon chicken salad or fresh, grilled salmon.

Edna Valley Vineyard Pinot Noir
(100% pinot noir)
Pair with gamey flavors such as duck, venison and wild mushroom pasta.

Edna Valley Vineyard Sauvignon Blanc
(100% sauvignon blanc)
Pair with raw oysters, crostinis with goat cheese or halibut with mango salsa.

Edna Valley Vineyard Syrah
(100% syrah)
Pair with a classic, spicy Santa Maria-Style tri-tip sandwich topped with fresh salsa.

Tastings
Open to the public daily, year-round

J. Lohr Vineyards & Wines

Paso Robles • Monterey County • Napa Valley

While names like Mondavi, Beringer and Chappellet were shaping the wine landscape of Napa Valley and California's more northern wine country, a handful of early pioneers were striving to establish a new outpost of winegrowing excellence on the Central Coast. One of the most visionary and influential of these individuals has been Jerry Lohr, the founder of J. Lohr Vineyards & Wines. As a winegrower, distinguished vintner and passionate advocate of Monterey County and Paso Robles, Jerry has helped to define quality on the Central Coast. At the same time, he has established J. Lohr Vineyards & Wines as one of the region's most acclaimed and iconic wineries.

Since its founding, J. Lohr Vineyards & Wines has focused on assembling one of the Central Coast's most storied estate programs. This program has been built on an important idea—that each grape varietal finds its best expression through a distinct combination of climate, soil type and location. With this in mind, J. Lohr planted its original 280 acres of grapes in Monterey County's Arroyo Seco appellation in the early 1970s. After helping to establish the Arroyo Seco as an ideal location for growing cool-climate white varietals— and later pinot noir—Jerry and his team set their sights on Paso Robles as the home for J. Lohr's warmer-climate, red-varietal vineyards. Confident of the region's potential to produce world-class red wines, in 1986 J. Lohr began planting cabernet sauvignon, merlot and other red grapes in the little-known Paso Robles region.

Top Left: Legendary founder Jerry Lohr and daughter, Cynthia, marketing vice president, enjoy a lighthearted moment in the barrel room.

Bottom Left: Brothers at work: Steve Lohr is executive vice president/chief operating officer of the family vineyards and Lawrence Lohr is the director of wine education.

Facing Page: J. Lohr Fog's Reach Vineyard in Arroyo Seco, Monterey County, has been known for growing cool-climate grapes since the 1970s.
Photographs by Paul Kirchner

Over the decades, J. Lohr's acclaimed portfolio of wines has helped to build the flavorful reputation of both regions, cementing Monterey County's status as a preeminent location for growing vibrant whites, and Paso's stature for producing voluptuous reds. At the same time, Jerry has gathered together a skilled and dedicated team of individuals, many of whom have been with J. Lohr for decades. This J. Lohr Winery team includes longtime winemaker and EVP-COO Jeff Meier, Monterey County Vineyard Manager Agapito Vazquez and Paso Robles Vineyard Manager Steve Carter, who collectively share over 65 years of experience. In the vineyards, J. Lohr's full-time vineyard crew averages approximately 10 years each with the company. All of this benefits J. Lohr with unprecedented levels of experience, consistency and continuity—factors that ensure great wines.

J. Lohr Vineyards & Wines has also been shaped by the passion and expertise of a second generation of the Lohr family. Daughter Cynthia leads corporate and product visibility efforts as vice president of marketing and son Steve is chief operating officer-executive vice president of J. Lohr Vineyards' growing vineyard holdings. Youngest son Lawrence

Above: Committed to sustainable grape growing and winemaking practices, J. Lohr owns more than 2,000 acres of estate vineyards in the Paso Robles AVA.
Photograph by Paul Kirchner

Right: J. Lohr Winery's red wine vinter Steve Peck and director of winemaking/winery EVP-COO Jeff Meier are an integral part of the J. Lohr team.
Photograph by Paul Kirchner

Facing Page Bottom: Sunshine welcomes visitors to an afternoon of wine tasting at the J. Lohr Paso Robles Wine Center.
Photograph by Ron Bez

Lohr advocates wine appreciation and history as director of wine education. Collectively, they have joined Jerry with an eye toward preserving family involvement in the winery—alongside J. Lohr's extended employee family—for generations to come. As part of this forward-looking vision, they have also helped to spearhead J. Lohr's commitment to sustainability in both winegrowing and winemaking.

A longtime advocate of such environmentally conscious practices as organic soil amendments, water conservation and composting, J. Lohr set a new industry standard when it unveiled its three-acre solar tracking array at its Paso Robles winemaking facility in 2009. As the largest tracking array in the wine industry, this system will reduce CO_2 emissions by almost 30,000 tons during its 25-year lifespan—the equivalent to not driving 97,000,000 miles.

Today, J. Lohr remains one of the few estate-focused wineries of its size, and one of the last substantial independents. Though it is operated with the loving care of a boutique winery, J. Lohr welcomes guests at two spectacular wine centers, one in San Jose and another in Paso Robles. In addition, J. Lohr's estate program cultivates more than 900 acres of cool-climate vineyards in Monterey County, 2,000 acres in Paso Robles,

Above: Stunning vistas with century-old oaks define J. Lohr's abundant Paso Robles vineyards.

Facing Page: The bright and airy J. Lohr San Jose Wine Center features a wide array of estate wines.
Photographs by Ron Bez

and 33 acres in Napa Valley. From this rich and diverse palette of sustainably farmed estate fruit, Jerry and the J. Lohr team work to craft wines that highlight bold, concentrated flavors and a vibrant sense of place. These vineyard-driven wines find their expression in three award-winning tiers: *J. Lohr Estates, J. Lohr Vineyard Series* and *J. Lohr Cuvée Series.*

Wine & Fare

J. Lohr Arroyo Vista Chardonnay
Pair with roasted chicken, pork or cream-based pasta dishes.

J. Lohr Hilltop Cabernet Sauvignon
Pair with beef bourguignon and hearty stews.

J. Lohr Fog's Reach Pinot Noir
Pair with grilled lamb or duck.

J. Lohr Carol's Vineyard Sauvignon Blanc
Pair with grilled or sautéed seafood and poultry.

Tastings
Open to the public daily, year-round

Jada Vineyard & Winery

Paso Robles

W hat does a fisherman's boat have to do with a Central Coast vineyard and winery? Jack Messina has a rich Italian heritage that goes back to his grandfather's homeland in Castellammare de Golfo, a Mediterranean village on Sicily's northern coast known as "castle by the sea." His grandfather had a fishing boat in the harbor and years later Jack saw the same type of boat with the name Jada on it, which made a lasting impression. Not surprisingly, when Jack and his wife Robyn founded Jada Vineyard & Winery, they aptly named the estate after that seaworthy boat reminiscent of his grandfather's.

Jack is a dedicated cardiac surgeon in Florida, but California dreaming led him to explore The Golden State for land to live on after retirement. He discovered the beautiful Templeton Gap ranch property, which had been a successful dry barley farm in the heart of Paso Robles. When neighbors told Jack that he had acquired acreage with ideal soil for grape-growing, he heeded their advice and planted his first estate vines in 1999. Jack's fruitful blocks soon became an abundant source of winegrapes and Jada Vineyard began supplying to top-notch wineries in the region. Once the first vines took root Jack was hooked on farming. He has since become a passionate grower of varietals perfect for crafting into fine Bordeaux and Rhône-style blends artfully aged in oaken casks. With well-respected winemaker Scott Hawley at his side since 2003, the enthusiastic vintners have created the award-winning XCV blend made from roussanne, viognier and grenache

Top Left: Jada Vineyard's sun-kissed block of cabernet sauvignon aspires to greatness.
Photograph by St. John Photography

Middle Left: Spring bud break holds the promise of award-winning wines to come.
Photograph by St. John Photography

Bottom Left: Jada's guest/pool house is gently nestled amid 14 acres of syrah.
Photograph by St. John Photography

Facing Page: Visitors are welcomed in style to Jada estate vineyards; its name is a nod to the owner's Italian roots.
Photograph by Maria Villano

blanc, the pure syrah whimsically named Jersey Girl in honor of Robyn and Hell's Kitchen crafted from spicy syrah, grenache, mourvèdre and tannat. Today, the limited-production winery produces 2,400 cases and is expected to peak at 5,000 cases annually in the next few years. Highly ranked by Stephen Tanzer and winning gold medals from the *San Francisco Chronicle*, Jada wines have enjoyed rave reviews since the first vintage in 2005. With such acclaim, the winery's Long Life wine club gladly ships bottles of its sought-after boutique wines to more than 1,300 members across the United States.

Jada wines are approachable and alluring, just as the destination vineyard: Upon arrival, dramatic entrance gates open, and the road curves to the right, lined with imported olive trees. Fruitless plum trees blossom in pink profusion along the frontage road. Winery visitors sample new vintages in an open-air tasting room while drinking in sweeping vineyard views. What once was a two-story barn with horse stables has been transformed into the tasting space

Top Left: The impressive gated entrance is just the beginning of the Jada experience.
Photograph by St. John Photography

Middle Left: A realized vision: Jada's Estrella cloned syrah encompasses row-upon-row of healthy vines.
Photograph by St. John Photography

Bottom Left: The contemporary tasting room features a relaxing open-air deck with magnificent views of the estate vineyard.
Photograph by St. John Photography

Facing Page: Hell's Kitchen is a spicy syrah blend, just one sophisticated selection from Jada's diverse wine portfolio.
Photograph by Maria Villano

and barrel room; its contemporary architectural design features an outdoor deck surrounded by century-old oaks. Gourmet cheese pairings are the house specialty, and guests enjoy new releases following a simple "wine-cheese-wine" method: Inhale the bouquet and sip to taste, have a bite of delicious artisan cheese, then taste the complex wine again to savor the palate-pleasing experience.

WINE & FARE

XVC 2008
(49% viognier, 26% roussanne, 25% grenache blanc)

Pair with slightly sweet Italian piave vecchio.

Hell's Kitchen
(40% estate syrah, 28% grenache, 16% mourvèdre, 16% tannat)

Pair with traditional French cheddar mimolette.

Jersey Girl
(100% syrah)

Pair with smooth and nutty Swiss grand cru gruyere.

Jack of Hearts
(45% estate cabernet sauvignon, 15% estate merlot, 40% estate petit verdot)

Pair with mild and rich Wisconsin dry jack.

Tastings
Open to the public Thursday through Monday, year-round

JUSTIN Vineyards & Winery

Paso Robles

Virtually an ambassador to the region, JUSTIN Vineyards & Winery near Paso Robles offers all of California's most appealing qualities. Forging ahead with winemaking when the Central Coast lived in the shadow of its Napa and Sonoma neighbors, JUSTIN made a name for itself nearly 20 years ago and has not let up since. The result of its efforts is a solid definition of what a Central Coast winery should be, setting the standard for all those who follow. And wine drinkers across the nation are catching on.

The names behind the bottles are Justin and Deborah Baldwin, who first planted vines in 1982 to begin their vision. Giving up investment and banking careers in Los Angeles, the couple took a risk when they purchased the 160-acre parcel of land just 15 miles west of Paso Robles. At the time, only eight wineries had been established in the area. Justin and Deborah slowly realized the possibilities of the geography, seeing a way to share a little piece of their world. Their resources also span the east and west side of the Paso Robles appellation to supplement on-site fruit. With topography that mimics the South of France and portions of Bordeaux, Paso Robles has a distinct flavor, as seen through JUSTIN's Bordeaux-style blends and single varietal bottlings.

The eclectic winery sits hidden just 13 miles off the Pacific Coast. Surrounding terrain offers a mix of textures and sights, with an unmistakable sense of place. The east side is flat and sandy with plenty of water while the west reveals verdant hillsides, little water

Top Left: The prime focus at JUSTIN Vineyards & Winery is the flagship Isosceles, a left bank Bordeaux-style blend of cabernet sauvignon, cabernet franc and merlot.
Photograph by W. Scott Loy

Bottom Left: Nightly dinners in Deborah's Room are an intimate and savory pleasure, complemented by the *Wine Spectator* Award of Excellence wine and champagne list.
Photograph by Chris Leschinsky

Facing Page: Guests of the JUST Inn can enjoy the vineyard view from the balcony and a complimentary bottle of handcrafted JUSTIN wine.
Photograph by Peter Malinowski

and rocky soils. The western portion of the region is where most of the winery grapes are sourced. The estate fruit, cabernet sauvignon, cabernet franc and merlot, make up most of the reserve portfolio. Hot days and cool nights blend with this topography to create strong tannic structures with spot-on acidity. And apparently connoisseurs around the world agree; wines like Isoceles, Justification, Savant, cabernet sauvignon and syrah sell in 27 countries and across the United States.

As the only winery on the Central Coast to do so, JUSTIN has a highly acclaimed restaurant, Deborah's Room, which offers weekend lunches and dinner nightly. Deborah's Room employs three full-time chefs who keep the menu perpetually fresh, with dishes like pan-seared day boat scallops, artisanal cheese boards and duck a l'orange. And what better

Top Left: The Isoceles Center is home to JUSTIN's wine caves and magnificent five-story Barrel Chai, where Guest Chef Dinners are held.
Photograph by Tracy Dauterman, JUSTIN Vineyards & Winery

Middle Left: JUST Inn's spacious Sussex suite exudes English charm replete with beautiful coffered ceilings, chintz fabric and fine antique furnishings.
Photograph by Peter Malinowski

Bottom Left: The winery's 18,000 square feet of naturally cool cave tunnels house handcrafted JUSTIN wine, where it slowly matures in traditional oak barrels.
Photograph by Chris Leschinsky

Facing Page: The Isoceles Library contains older vintages of sought-after Isoceles available for purchase only through the special tour program.
Photograph by Chris Leschinsky

lodgings would suit a trip to the winery than the JUST Inn Bed & Breakfast? The European-style rooms offer interiors of various regions, like Bordeaux, Tuscany and Sussex. From accommodations to cuisine to the finest wines, JUSTIN Vineyards & Winery prides itself on delivering an all-around experience to guests, showing off the virtues of the Central Coast.

JUSTIN

ISOSCELES
Reserve

PASO ROBLES

WINE & FARE

Chardonnay

Pair with poultry and seafood dishes like Dover sole in a white wine cream sauce, Parmesan-crusted chicken and lobster entrees. Bel Paese, Cambozola, Pave, Dry Jack, Pecorino and Provolone are perfect matches as well.

Isosceles

Match this wine with cheeses like Abbaye de Belloc, Danish blue, aged Gouda, Reblochon and San Andreas. Grilled steaks, filet mignon and venison also pair well.

Syrah

Pair with properly seasoned roasted, grilled or sautéed meats; poultry and game. Ideal dishes include herb-roasted duck or chicken and veal osso bucco. Try sharp Cheddar, Edam and Gouda.

Reserve Tempranillo

Pair with Argentinean spices, Spanish tapas, lamb, slow-cooked beef stew, grilled meats, Cheddar, Gouda and Jarlsberg.

Tastings
Open to the public daily, year-round

L'Aventure

Paso Robles

When Frenchman and vigneron Stephan Asseo scouted the world for the perfect terroir seeking to escape strict winemaking regulations imposed in his native country, his heart was captured by beautiful Paso Robles, California. After 17 years of winemaking in the renowned Bordeaux region, Stephan pulled up stakes and brought his young family on a grand adventure to America, ultimately cultivating the perfect piece of land in Paso Robles. Stephan purchased 120 acres of steep rolling hills on the west side where the soils were quite unique with great agricultural potential; since acquiring the property he planted 40 blocks on 60 acres and built the exclusive L'Aventure winery in 1998. Discovering this select terroir has offered Stephan the opportunity to experience a newfound freedom of creativity for his life's passion.

Today Stephan is approaching three decades as a seasoned vigneron and has gained a deep understanding: Growing vines on world-class terroir equates to superior fruit, resulting in fine wines of exemplary quality. His trademark growing philosophy is to densely plant 2,100 vines per acre—a rarity in the industry—where the vines' competitive nature gives rise to prized low-yield harvests. L'Aventure is considered the Central Coast's haute couture winery, and its estate wine portfolio includes handcrafted, French oak-aged red blends, like the award-winning Optimus and Estate Cuvée, with indescribable complexities and nuances born from the grapes grown on Stephan's beloved vineyard. A purist, Stephan is dedicated to his precious terroir so rich in history; he is a dedicated steward of the land and true artist transforming each fruitful vine into one bottle of glorious wine.

Top Left: Founder and vigneron Stephan Asseo oversees fruitful vineyards and passionately crafts delicious red wines.
Photograph by Maria Villano.

Middle Left: The rustic L'Aventure sign at the entry gate marks Stephan's precious terroir.
Photograph by Maria Villano

Bottom Left: Elegant script on the L'Aventure label accents Stephan's award-winning wines in classic French style.
Photograph by Chandler Smiley

Facing Page: Magnificent vistas capture the charming L'Aventure estate vineyard and winery nestled in the hills.
Photograph by Chandler Smiley

Maloy O'Neill Vineyards

Paso Robles

"When Irish Eyes Are Smiling" is a song that cherishes the warm personalities, lightheartedness and endearing spirit of those with ancestral roots in Ireland. Shannon O'Neill and Maureen Maloy share this heritage and their Irish-American names are united as proud owners of Maloy O'Neill Vineyards located in beautiful Paso Robles. Shannon, head winemaker, together with Maureen, CEO, marketing and events director as well as mom, have combined their individual family crests on each precious bottle to impress upon wine enthusiasts their dedication to handcrafted quality that goes into the more than 36 different wines produced by the estate vineyard each year. Besides their Irish ancestry, Shannon has deep Italian roots and Maureen is half French so their regional winemaking reflects a decidedly international flair.

The 150-acre O'Neill Vineyard was originally established in 1982. A second piece of land, Maloy-O'Neill Vineyard, was acquired by Maureen and Shannon in 1999 to become the estate's premier commercial vintage, and in 2000 their Syrah Private Reserve took home the winery's first industry accolade. An extensive list of lesser-known and ever popular estate-bottled varietals include chardonnay, cabernet sauvignon, cabernet franc, merlot, petite sirah, pinot noir, sangiovese, malbec, tempranillo, malvasia bianca, muscat blanc, lagrein, syrah and zinfandel. Renowned especially for big, concentrated red wines with intense character, the small lot, family-owned winery creates up to 5,000 cases of estate-grown varietals that are distributed domestically.

Top Left: Shannon and Maureen O'Neill founded their namesake estate winery together.
Photograph by Lifetouch

Middle Left: Handcrafted wines possess traditional Old World quality and bear the Maloy O'Neill family crest.
Photograph by M.J. Wickham

Bottom Left: The tasting list at Maloy O'Neill changes monthly to showcase the 36 different lots of each vintage before they sell out.
Photograph by M.J. Wickham

Facing Page: An oak tree-lined creek bed cuts through the vineyard's chalky, sandy loam terroir.
Photograph by M.J. Wickham

Once an almond orchard planted in 1907 called Windy Hill, the boutique winery's vineyards have grown since the early days in Paso Robles to encompass hundreds of rolling and rocky acres. The region's adverse, nutrient-deficient soil conditions and broad diurnal temperature flux "cause the vines to suffer" as the old French saying goes, which vintners believe is part of the secret to creating greatness in the wines this appellation produces. Today the traditional English- and French Country-inspired main winery and tasting room are situated on prime property with stunning panoramic views of the vineyards. The manicured grounds have fountains and a breathtaking picnic area. The winery has become the region's top-rated venue for weddings and special events as well as educational courses. The married owners-vintners, Maureen and Shannon, met while attending the University of California at Davis where they earned valuable credentials, later enriched with more than 20 years of winemaking experience. The owners love to share their life's passion of artisan winemaking, as well as their vast knowledge of viticulture with tourists and locals alike.

Celebrating a milestone of more than 10 years in the winemaking business, Shannon and Maureen personally welcome winery guests, whether novice or collector, to experience the handcrafted distinction of Maloy O'Neill Vineyards. These award-winning producers create some of the highest quality, limited-quantity estate wines in the region and have earned

Top Left: Winemaker and owner Shannon O'Neill punches down in a half-ton MacroBin, highlighting how all of the winery's processes are done by hand.

Bottom Left: Thirteen beautiful acres of cabernet sauvignon produce fruitful yields on the Maloy O'Neill Vineyards' Windy Hill Estate.

Facing Page: The Maloy O'Neill property is a fabulous venue for special events with its breathtaking, panoramic hilltop views and well-appointed tasting room.
Photographs by M.J. Wickham

more than 50 medals in the last several years. Their exclusive Cellar Club invites members to sample newly released wines on a quarterly delivery basis as a convenient way to enjoy Maloy O'Neill wines year-round. The down to earth, yet sophisticated family business has one more surprise: The winery's beloved, red-haired mascot Tootsie, an Irish wolfhound and airedale mix, greets guests with her irresistible, canine charm. Tootsie is also a local hero, having gained national attention by saving two lives. She was featured with her heroic story in *Wine Dogs USA 2*, and was also picked for the cover of the 2009 *Wine Dogs USA* calendar.

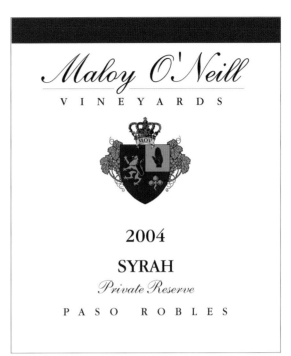

WINE & FARE

Maloy O'Neill Gioi
(65% sangiovese, 25% cabernet sauvignon, 10% merlot)

Pair with great pizza and pasta dishes like lasagne and ravioli or eggplant parmesan.

Maloy O'Neill Syrah Private Reserve
(100% syrah)

Pair with grilled meats, crown roast, pork and lamb, spicy sausages and hard cheeses.

Maloy O'Neill Cabernet Sauvignon
(100% cabernet sauvignon)

Pair with filet mignon, pot roast, lamb chops, pasta dishes and beef bourguignon.

Tastings
Open to the public Thursday through Monday or by appointment, year-round

Peachy Canyon Winery

Templeton

Growing up in San Diego County as the son of a U.S. Navy pilot, Doug Beckett lived amid the Southern California surfside culture. Academically inclined and driven, he earned his bachelor's degree in business administration and went on to receive his master's in psychology, which led to teaching and work as a high school counselor. Doug married his college sweetheart Nancy, a professional dancer and instructor. Proud parents of two sons, Josh and Jake, the couple brought their honor roll students northward for a decidedly different California upbringing. The family's move came in 1982, and the founding vintner couple established Peachy Canyon Winery seven years later in the Paso Robles appellation.

The Becketts took several trips to the Central Coast in search of the perfect place to live; they loved antique hunting and enjoyed the spirited California lifestyle along the way as they traveled up Pacific Coast Highway in Doug's favorite 1970s Volkswagen Bus. The pair discovered an old home on beautiful San Luis Obispo County land, a turn-of-the-century New England farmhouse; the family recreated the home based on the original and started anew. Industrious people, Doug became a skilled carpenter while Nancy opened her illustrious dance studio.

Their earliest inspiration stemmed from meeting Pat Wheeler of Tobias Vineyards and the couple began making wine at home in the evenings. For five years the neighbors partnered—Doug and Nancy gleaned experience in the winemaking business until their private label was born in 1988. Local Chris Johnson lent Doug 20 used barrels and was

Top Left: A welcoming, hand-lettered banner marks the entrance to Peachy Canyon Winery's official tasting room.

Bottom Left: Bursting with potential, a cluster of ripe zinfandel grapes is ready to be picked at Old School House Estate Vineyard.

Facing Page: Old School House Estate Vineyard enjoys cool, sun-drenched days—the perfect climate for growing fruitful yields.
Photographs by Steve E. Miller

fronted six tons of zinfandel grapes from the famed Benito Dusi vineyard to get them started, and they emerged with a 500-case venture in 1990 with the premiere release of zinfandel, the family winery's specialty. From this humble beginning, the winery has evolved to produce more than 85,000 cases of internationally known zinfandel, cabernet, merlot and special blends. Each wine is released in the peak of its youth so enthusiasts can enjoy wines young or cellar them for a later date. Highly select allocated wines and under-600-cases-per-release wines are also part of their stellar portfolio.

A small loyal crew handpicks and hand-sorts the best fruit while select workers hand-prune and harvest the prized vineyards. Sensitive to the environment, all Peachy Canyon estate vineyards are farmed using advanced sustainable practices. Today the award-winning Peachy Canyon Winery handcrafted brand is widely distributed in 49 states, Europe, the Pacific Rim and throughout Canada.

Doug became one of the first members of the Paso Robles Vintners and Growers Association and an original founder of the region's noteworthy Wine Festival. At the time Peachy Canyon was established

Top Left: An outdoor gazebo and picnic area invites alfresco sipping at the Old School House tasting room.

Bottom Left: The cozy tasting room is filled with delicious wines and fabulous gifts to delight the novice or connoisseur.

Facing Page Top: Exhibiting 19th-century architecture, the charming Old School House tasting room is nestled amid Peachy Canyon's 200-acre estate vineyards.

Facing Page Bottom: Peachy Canyon's close family of vintners includes Josh and Gibsey Beckett with daughters Ava and Sydney, founders Doug and Nancy Beckett, and Jake and Dawn Beckett with sons Braydon and Logan.
Photographs by Steve E. Miller

there were only 11 area wineries. The world-recognized Paso Robles AVA now has nearly 200 wineries, but Peachy Canyon was one of the first family-owned and operated wineries in the region. Doug's eldest, Josh Beckett has served as head winemaker for nearly a decade, having studied with world-acclaimed vintners from France to Australia. Jake Beckett handles sales throughout the United States and also holds the role of vineyard manager when he is not on the road. With Doug as CEO, all are instrumental in the growing of grapes and the growth of the estate itself, having acquired more than 100 acres encompassing four vineyards: Snow Vineyard in a warm westside location, Old Schoolhouse Vineyard in the coolest region of Templeton Gap, Mustang Springs Ranch planted with 55-year-old zinfandel and Mustard Creek Vineyard, which boasts the welcoming guest cottage. Each distinct vineyard has its own climate and terroir characteristics to grow very different grapes.

One historic structure on Old Schoolhouse Vineyard estate has become the pride and joy of Peachy Canyon Winery. The circa-1886 schoolhouse was transformed into a quaint place for daily tastings with a fine gift shop; it is now a landmark attraction on tours. The property also offers an old-fashioned gazebo and park-like picnic area bordered by rolling vineyards and mature oak trees.

Above Left: The historic Old School House landmark is an endearing part of the destination winery.

Above Right: One scarecrow stands guard over the vineyard where traditional hand pruning and harvesting techniques are employed.

Facing Page:Handcrafted by winemaker Josh Beckett, DeVine cabernet sauvignon is one of the winery's classic reds and the perfect gourmet accompaniment.
Photographs by Steve E. Miller

A labor of love, winemaking is an art form and way of life by design for the Beckett family. Doug sums up his simple formula for success: "All one needs is a vision and discerning palate to make great wines for family, friends and fans." This second-generation winery involves the entire family living and working together in a neighborly community—an idyllic lifestyle for Doug and Nancy, grown children Josh and Jake with their wives and the Beckett grandkids.

WINE & FARE

Peachy Canyon Viognier
Pair with butter poached shellfish and fresh oysters.

Peachy Canyon Zinfandel
Pair with traditional barbecue dishes and strong blue cheeses.

Peachy Canyon Petite Sirah
Pair with rich gamey dishes, roasted rack of lamb or a dark chocolate dessert.

Peachy Canyon Para Siempre
Pair with braised short ribs or smoked and cured meats.

Tastings
Open to the public daily, year-round

Pear Valley Vineyard & Winery

Paso Robles

While stationed on a U.S. army base in Germany after his '60s tour of duty, Tom Maas got a true taste of inspiration being surrounded by scenic country vineyards and distinctive wineries. He promised himself that one day he would follow his passion, control his destiny and have a vineyard and winery back home in California. Tom made his dream a reality. He planted his first block of grapevines in San Luis Obispo County on his 115-acre estate soon after raising a family with wife Kathleen. Pear Valley Vineyard & Winery was established in 1997, and today these dedicated Paso Robles AVA vintners and growers share a mission to create delightful regional wines while conducting sustainable farming practices with a no-waste philosophy in mind.

Pear Valley Vineyard was once a pear orchard nurtured on remarkable agricultural soils. Seizing the opportunity, Tom recognized the perfect place for grape-growing success to be in his own fertile backyard. UC Davis alumnus and winemaker James Hendon partnered with the Maas family and together they are keenly dedicated to green practices, constantly working toward a minimal carbon footprint as they produce some of the region's most talked about and approachable wines.

Tom and James make wine where it really begins, in the vineyards, designing drinkable wines to be enjoyed that truly respect the essence of the land. Wines are derived from varietals grown in three limited-production vineyards, including the Mission Almond Estate, Pear Valley and Union Road Estates. James has at his fingertips premium fruit harvests of French and Italian descent: pinot noir, malbec, chardonnay, mourvèdre, merlot,

Top Left: Visitors especially enjoy wine on the patio with an expansive view of Paso Robles.
Photograph by Becky Sloat Photography

Middle Left: Anticipation grows as guests await a celebration in the event room on the Pear Valley estate.
Photograph by Pear Valley Vineyard & Winery

Bottom Left: An approach through the vineyards reveals warm, earth-toned buildings inspired by the owners' Tuscan sojourns.
Photograph by Becky Sloat Photography

Facing Page: Grace and beauty in the garden create an ambience ideal for sipping new vintages.
Photograph by Becky Sloat Photography

cabernet franc, zinfandel, cabernet sauvignon, syrah, grenache, petit verdot, aglianico and moscato. The winery's most unique vintage is named "Distraction" paying lighthearted homage to Tom's obvious passion; it is a Bordeaux-style blend that has turned out to be the crème de la crème of Pear Valley's wine portfolio. The limited-production boutique winery renders 4,000 cases of handcrafted varietals and blends per year, and the vintners prefer to keep it that way. James employs traditional Old World winemaking methods, yet utilizes the latest lab tools and technology, then properly ages wine in natural oak barrels; he loves melding art and science. "It's about growing the purest grapes with just the right balance of acids and sugars. I rely on what nature intended and try not to interfere with perfection," avers James.

An extension of the proprietors' genuine warmth and determined eco-consciousness, the energy-efficient and environmentally sound winery features a tasting room space that is open and inviting. Guests can also enjoy a bottle of artisan wine with their picnic lunches out on the patio overlooking some of nature's most mesmerizing vineyard sunsets. Tours are available upon request, and special events run the

Top Left: Early morning tranquility blankets the tasting room before guests arrive for a lively experience.
Photograph by Pear Valley Vineyard & Winery

Middle Left: The winery building, bathed in Central Coast sunlight, holds the heart of the winemaking process.
Photograph by Pear Valley Vineyard & Winery

Bottom Left: Passionate vintners Tom and Kathleen Maas share a commitment to sustainable viticulture practices.
Photograph by Becky Sloat Photography

Facing Page: Delicious, award-winning wines are born from premium fruit grown on Pear Valley's three vineyards.
Photograph by Pear Valley Vineyard & Winery

gamut from casual evenings starring James on acoustic guitar to celebratory harvest festivals and convivial private tastings. Creating unique vintages that reflect vibrant fruit nourished by ancient soils under ideal climate conditions while leaving little impact on the environment, is the impetus behind Pear Valley Vineyard & Winery. Inspired by a coveted terroir, the Maas family cordially offers novice wine drinkers, enthusiasts and connoisseurs a taste of the naturally good life captured in each flavorful bottle of Pear Valley wine.

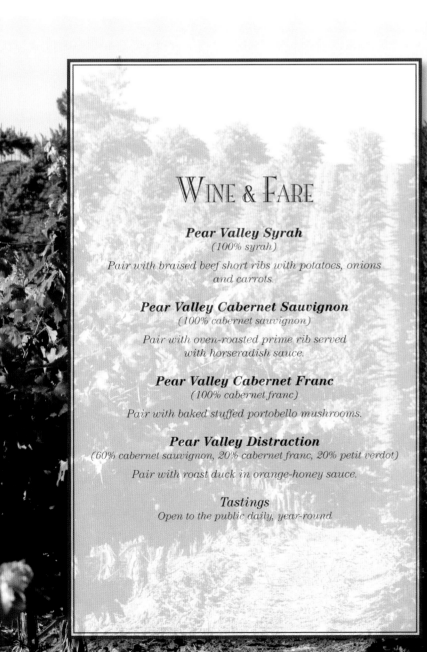

WINE & FARE

Pear Valley Syrah
(100% syrah)

Pair with braised beef short ribs with potatoes, onions and carrots.

Pear Valley Cabernet Sauvignon
(100% cabernet sauvignon)

Pair with oven-roasted prime rib served with horseradish sauce.

Pear Valley Cabernet Franc
(100% cabernet franc)

Pair with baked stuffed portobello mushrooms.

Pear Valley Distraction
(60% cabernet sauvignon, 20% cabernet franc, 20% petit verdot)

Pair with roast duck in orange-honey sauce.

Tastings
Open to the public daily, year-round

Robert Hall Winery

Paso Robles

Inspired by a trip to France in the 1970s, Robert L. Hall returned with a passion for wine and a desire to recreate what he had experienced visiting the Rhône Valley. Robert and Margaret visited and researched each U.S. winegrowing region, and in the early '90s discovered the Paso Robles appellation of the Central Coast. This exceptional California growing region possesses the rolling terroir and ideal Mediterranean-like climate with warm days and cool nights reminiscent of the world-renowned Rhône Valley. Robert's journey to becoming a respected vintner came after successful years as an entrepreneur. Embarking on his new venture he put his heart and soul into growing grapes and has since created award-winning wines that embody the essence of Paso Robles.

Robert Hall Winery honors Old World winemaking traditions yet utilizes the latest technology and eco-sensitive viticultural methods. The winery has proudly achieved the Sustainability in Practice (SIP)™ certification for its more than 300-acre Hall Ranch, which has four sustainably farmed vineyards: Home Vineyard, Terrace Vineyard, Bench Vineyard and Brady Vineyard. This family-owned winery painstakingly practices environmentally sustainable agricultural methods to conserve precious natural resources.

Top Left: Natural wine corks seal all Robert Hall wines.

Middle Left: An impressive artisan-crafted chandelier is suspended in the winery creating a celebratory ambience. There are three featured chandeliers to be seen in the tasting room, tower and Meritage Room.

Bottom Left: The vine's healthy cabernet sauvignon grape leaf and tendril promises a fruitful yield.

Facing Page: Hall Ranch's Bench Vineyard as viewed from the garden terrace seems to go on and on. All estate vineyards grown on Hall Ranch have achieved Sustainability in Practice™ certification.
Photographs by Maria Villano

Robert Hall winemaker and director Don Brady's mission is to "nurture the land and coax from it the finest fruit possible through advanced viticulture practices on the expansive Hall Ranch." Don selects from a myriad of Rhône and Bordeaux varietals derived from each vineyard, grapes with distinctive character expressing unique nuances. The estate vineyards are a veritable showcase of the best of the Paso Robles AVA. Crafting wines of distinction by blending different grapes, subtleties are captured so those who discover Robert Hall wines can taste the warmth and vitality of California's enchanting Central Coast. Years of hard work and infinite attention to detail are invested in every bottle, with integrity the main ingredient.

From vineyard tours to private barrel tastings, the Robert Hall tasting room and hospitality center— where samples are sipped and local artists exhibit their original work—embraces guests with a feeling of the relaxed California lifestyle. This state-of-the-art destination winery also boasts 19,000 square feet of underground wine caverns—testament to the founder's contribution in developing California's most exciting wine region. Visitors can expect a truly unique experience on a guided educational tour of the inner sanctum where Robert Hall wines mature in premium oak barrels. In addition to the winery's impressive cavern, the hospitality center features a Meritage Room and wine library where

Top Left: The Meritage Room is a perfect setting for elegant wine dinners, special events and business conferences.
Photograph by Kenneth Morgan

Middle Left: The Robert Hall Winery hospitality center invites guests to taste new vintages and enjoy the relaxing winery experience.
Photograph by Maria Villano

Bottom Left: A scenic vista encompasses the courtyard with its reflecting pool and mahogany beam design, leading visitors to the winery's landmark fountain.
Photograph by Maria Villano

Facing Page: The renowned proprietary blend, Rhône de Robles, is a delicious mélange of grenache, syrah, cinsaut and counoise characterized by soft, velvety tannins with a burst of berry fruit.
Photograph by Josh Kimball

intimate tastings and enlightening seminars are hosted. The open-air amphitheater and garden terrace are venues for lively sunset concerts, and the winery courtyard, replete with fountain, reflecting pool and a lovely rose garden, adds a touch of romance to the inviting setting. And, in keeping with the winery's engaging spirit, guests are always welcome to participate in a leisurely game of bocce ball or simply enjoy a gourmet picnic on the beautiful grounds.

WINE & FARE

Robert Hall Rose de Robles
Pair with pork tenderloin served with fresh watermelon salsa.

Robert Hall Rhône de Robles
Pair with balsamic vinegar and rosemary marinated Florentine steak.

Robert Hall Cabernet Sauvignon
Pair with spareribs seasoned with mustard, garlic and marinade.

Robert Hall Vintage Port
Pair with poached pears topped with crumbled blue cheese and toasted walnuts.

Tastings
Open to the public daily, year-round

Sculpterra Winery & Sculpture Garden

Paso Robles

What emerges when fine wine and fine art come together? A natural fusion of creativity that stirs the senses. The brainchild of Dr. Warren Frankel, Sculpterra Winery & Sculpture Garden is nestled in the scenic Linne Valley—just three miles east of Paso Robles—where a unique melding of wine and art lives in radiant harmony.

On a visit to Oslo, Norway, 18-year-old Warren was inspired by beautiful Frogner Park, a public sculpture garden, and an innovative idea was born. A passionate art collector, Warren envisioned the same lush park setting where wine-lovers could relax and sip new vintages while surrounded by great sculpture. Thirty years later, he commissioned renowned American sculptor John Jagger to create several incredible pieces, now permanent installations on the Sculpterra property. Ironwork by Robert C. Bentley greets guests at the entry gate, while Jagger's centerpiece granite *Golden Morning* stretch cat—with her impressive 14-foot-high, 17,000-pound feline pose—certainly catches your attention. A dozen monumental bronzes by Jagger are installed on the grounds and select miniature sculptures are displayed in the tasting room.

Warren acquired his beloved property in 1979, first cultivating cabernet sauvignon grapes and pistachio trees, and then planting most of the 120 acres of grapevines in 1997; his vineyards had already become an established source for premium fruit sold to boutique wineries throughout Napa Valley and along the Central Coast. Sculpterra's terroir is reminiscent of the Medoc-Graves region of Bordeaux, thus classic cabernet

Top Left: *Golden Morning* stretch cat is the winery's magnificent entry sculpture created by John Jagger, adorned with bronze whiskers and bronze claws.

Middle Left: *Puma*, a 15-foot-long sculpture carved from solid granite, is the largest art piece of this specific granite in the world. The stunning sculpture by John Jagger weighs 20,000 pounds.

Bottom Left: *Mammoth* was carved from granite and weighs 16,000 pounds. Sculptor John Jagger exposes the inner animal to express its power and movement; tusks are pearl white granite with tips of bronze.

Facing Page: *Yahoo!* is a 15-foot-high, hand-welded bucking horse weighing over 2,000 pounds. Constructed by sculptor John Jagger, one drop of bronze at a time was laid over the bronze framework.
Photographs by Bruce Woodworth

sauvignon was the first success. Today the vineyards boast thriving blocks of cabernet sauvignon, merlot, zinfandel, viognier, mourvédre, petite sirah, pinot noir, primitivo and cabernet franc. The region's complex soils and rare micro-climate contribute to growing the best winegrapes.

Sculpterra's premiere vintage was crafted in 2005. The winery has received numerous medals and earned high accolades from judges for its refined vintages. Warren's son, Paul Frankel, inherited his father's passion for the wine business and went on to earn his bachelor's degree in winemaking and viticulture at Cal Poly with the goal of becoming Sculpterra's resident vintner and viticulturist upon graduation; his debut year as winemaker was 2008. He blogs daily about wine adventures, blending art and science, the challenges of grape growing, nuances of the craft, and his fulfilling life on the vineyards. Paul grew up on the land, fell in love with wine country culture and is dedicated to making the best varietals and blends from his family's estate vineyard. "Our wines are perfect to drink now, but they also age gracefully," says Paul. Handcrafting traditional French-style wines, Paul is a minimalist who treats the fruit delicately with very little interference so the wines are pure expressions. His handmade wines possess a uniform, round mouth feel with full form that speaks to the region, all in keeping with the family philosophy. "We sculpt the land. We don't create it, but bring out the best of its natural fruit. God creates the grapes and we simply help to reveal His creation in our wines," says Warren.

Top Left: An enriching tasting room experience awaits guests at Sculpterra Winery & Sculpture Garden.

Bottom Left: Warren and Katherine Frankel enjoy horseback riding while inspecting their estate vineyards.

Facing Page: The inspiring view from the lookout point shows estate cabernet sauvignon on to Sculpterra's tasting room and entrance.
Photographs by Bruce Woodworth

Dr. Frankel's passion is to unite wine with art while giving support to His Healing Hands, a medical missionary non-profit organization that he co-founded. This humanitarian organization sends out medical missionary teams of physicians to treat impoverished people and victims of natural disasters around the globe. A portion of Sculpterra Winery proceeds goes to supporting this cause. Warren has even written a book on the subject of his heartfelt mission trips. Wine, art and healing is the true meaning behind Sculpterra. Visitors on tour often sit atop Warren's Vista Point to experience the richness of the oak-laden terroir, as they savor fruit of the vine and work of human hands in every sip.

WINE & FARE

Sculpterra 2008 Viognier
Pair with Asian pear and fresh, local goat cheese wrapped with prosciutto.

Sculpterra 2005 Cabernet Sauvignon
Pair with spicy ahi tuna tartare in a crispy cup.

Sculpterra 2007 Syrah
Pair with portobellini filled with wild mushroom duxelle, topped with parmesan cheese gratine.

Sculpterra 2007 Statuesque
Pair with smoked duck on a bed of fresh cherry chutney with a dot of wine reduction, served on a fresh baguette.

Tastings
Open to the public daily, year-round

Sextant Wines/10knots Cellars

San Luis Obispo

Much of winemaking is about getting your bearings straight. Navigating to the right site, of course, will determine your terroir and will ultimately determine the capacity for grape expression. Once there, you explore for perfect lots. The rest is a path of discovery, an epic search for potable treasure. At least this is how the Stollers view the adventure of winemaking. With Sextant Wines, the winemakers have begun a journey that exemplifies the American spirit of determination. "It's very tough work," says Craig Stoller, Sextant's proprietor; "You have to love it to do it." And by taking their passion a little bit further, the Stollers have managed to invigorate California's Central Coast with a new winemaking character.

Though first planting Sextant's vines in 2003, Craig and Nancy Stoller have been rooted in the wine industry for quite a while. The family owns and operates Sunridge Nurseries, an all but ubiquitous player in the region's vineyards that has dedicated years of perfecting vine growth to earn trust and competence in wine country, guaranteeing that the nursery is truly where the vintage begins. That first planting, in fact, was intended to supply wineries with cuttings; though the typical nursery method is to let the fruit drop while clones are developing, Nancy and Craig decided to utilize the spoils. The couple's fascination with Bordeaux-style wines led them to plant as many zinfandel clones as they could find, including some new varieties from ENTAV, the French governmental agency that validates the origin and authenticity of winegrape clones. This was Sextant's Templeton vineyard, and the lot proved unmatched in terroir, a remarkably adept spot for the Old World clones. According to Craig: "I thought it would be great to see what these clones could do. I just didn't think it would happen so soon."

Top Left: Clusters of zinfandel ripen in Sextant's Templeton vineyard.
Photograph by John Hensley, Sextant Wine Club Member

Bottom Left: Through Sextant, Nancy and Craig Stoller celebrate life and live their dream.
Photograph by Amanda Frank, Frankly Yours Photography

Facing Page: San Luis Obispo is home to Sextant Wines/10knots Cellars' tasting room and hospitality center.
Photograph by Peter Malinowski

To really hit at the Bordeaux style, the Stollers, and winemaker Kevin Riley, blend so that layers of complexity become apparent. In that region in France, the climate forces blending because the grapes never fully ripen. However, here, on the Central Coast, they do, giving Sextant the perfect array of rich, full-bodied flavors. Much of this is about timing: You have to know precisely when to harvest grapes and precisely when to blend. For Sextant, a tide of accolades and critical acclaim soon came flooding in, with wine scores in the 90s from the likes of Robert Parker Jr. of *The Wine Advocate, Wine Enthusiast* and *Wine Spectator* to name a few. Blending with syrah, petite sirah or mourvèdre, these zinfandels—like the stellar Night Watch or the inviting Wheelhouse—certainly beg the question, "Did I just kill that whole bottle?"

As Nancy and Craig quickly became renowned for their zinfandels, their travels through Europe revealed a new love for Rhône varietals. The result was a bevy of accolades and awards for these Rhône wines, including double golds at both the Florida State and the San Francisco International Wine competitions. Their fascination with the ocean resurfaced once again with the release of their second label, 10knots Cellars.

Top Left: A glimpse of Old Edna is enjoyed from the MacGregor vineyard.
Photograph by John Hensley, Sextant Wine Club Member

Middle Left: The perfect scene: a little Sextant, 10knots and a splash of beach.
Photograph by Amanda Frank, Frankly Yours Photography

Bottom Left: The tasting room and hospitality center welcome visitors from around the world.
Photograph by Peter Malinowski

Facing Page: Kamal and Night Watch are treasured Sextant reserve wines.
Photograph by Peter Malinowski

This is propelled discovery. The Stoller family's wanderlust of the mind and the mouth certainly steers the Sextant ship. Herman Melville once wrote of "that thingumbob sextant perplexing eyes and hands." Well, thanks to these winemakers, we can now add the palate.

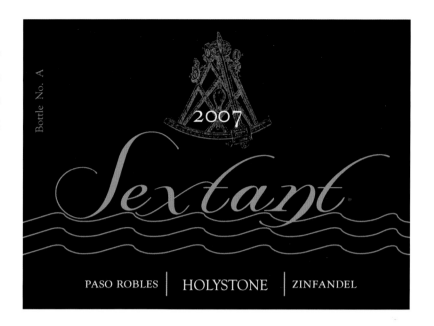

WINE & FARE

Sextant Wheelhouse Zinfandel
(81% zinfandel, 16% syrah, 2% petite sirah, 1% mourvèdre)

Pair with lamb sliders with caramelized shallots, gruyère cheese and dijon aioli.

Sextant Night Watch Proprietary Red
(45% petite sirah, 32% zinfandel, 19% syrah, 4% grenache)

Pair with porcini-rubbed filet mignon with truffle butter, served over whipped root vegetables.

10knots Beachcomber White Rhône
(61% viognier, 24% grenache blanc, 12% roussanne, 3% marsanne)

Pair with coconut crusted prawns over baby greens drizzled with warm, citrus-honey vinaigrette.

Sextant Santa Lucia Highlands Chardonnay
(100% chardonnay)

Pair with seared scallops served over arugula-endive salad with citrus herbs.

Tastings
Open to the public daily, year-round

Silver Horse
Vineyard and Winery

San Miguel

S ometimes the way to discover exciting wines is to hear about them right from the horse's mouth. "Sharing good wine with friends and telling stories around the dinner table is the best method for connecting with wine lovers," says Stephen Kroener, head winemaker and co-owner of Silver Horse Vineyard and Winery.

The family owned and operated vineyard and winery goes back three generations to Grandpa Kroener, who made wine for relatives and friends at the original homestead in LA County. Years later in 1996, son Jim Kroener took the idea further by acquiring a sprawling San Miguel property with 80 acres of thoroughbred horse stables and vineyards in Pleasant Valley—1,000 feet high on a hilltop amid the fertile Paso Robles AVA. Stephen's winemaking passion was inspired by times spent with his grandfather, tasting new wines in the cellar where the oaky scent of aging vintages made an unforgettable impression. Stephen strives to capture traditional family values and quality in his artisan wines, and each drop of Silver Horse expresses the essence of his storied vintner heritage. The Kroener family vision unfolded again, as Stephen joined his father to update Silver Horse winery, planning construction of an all new winery-tasting facility that came to fruition in 2005.

Silver Horse is praised for having one of the best views of the Central Coast's wine country with vistas of bucolic splendor. A rural destination, the vineyard and winery produces Rhône-style, Bordeaux and Spanish varietals and blends, all creatively handcrafted by Stephen. The rich agricultural region boasts soils and a maritime climate ideal for growing

Top Left: The iconic sculptural logo for Silver Horse Winery is "The S'orse."

Bottom Left: Budding petit verdot vines promise great Bordeaux-style blends.

Facing Page: Picturesque Pleasant Valley can be viewed from one of many patios at Silver Horse.
Photographs by Maria Villano

premium grapes, and Silver Horse's estate vineyard yields malbec, petit verdot, cabernet sauvignon, syrah, tempranillo and grenache. Albarino, merlot and petite syrah are sourced from area vineyards. This micro-boutique winery lives up to its philosophy of crafting eclectic wines that are genuinely food-friendly, age-worthy and highly sought after. Their S'orce Wine Club has attracted a cult following, and the winery enjoys sold-out vintages after bottling each year. S'orce Wine Club got its name for a reason: Silver Horse is a natural "source" for good fruit, good wines and good times. Silver Horse Winery produces fewer than 2,000 cases annually, derived strictly from estate fruit harvests, making each enjoyable bottle a true celebration of the land.

Aside from the gorgeous 360-degree views, guests experience a hacienda-style tasting room with its cozy, relaxed atmosphere. Four friendly dogs form the meet-and-greet team, licking and wagging their way through tastings. Tour visitors get a hands-on experience from a welcoming staff, knowledgeable in both wine and the history of the region. Stephen, the resident chef, often creates gourmet fare—dishes inspired by his mother Suzanne made exclusively for wine club members—using the winery's wood-fired oven. A local landmark, the winery holds weddings and social events year-round in its beautiful 3,000-square-foot reception facility. The family of

Top Left: Silver Horse Winery attracts visitors to its beautiful hacienda tasting room and event facility.

Middle Left: Estate cabernet sauvignon vines produce some of the best wines in the Paso Robles AVA.

Bottom Left: The cozy tasting room is not only welcoming to guests but also gives a behind-the-scenes look at the inner workings of the winery.

Facing Page: Exquisite wines are best enjoyed when surrounded by a classic vineyard and winery setting.
Photographs by Maria Villano

vintners believes in the personal touch; even winemaker dinners in private homes can be arranged, where Stephen uncorks a bottle of Silver Horse, then prepares a delectable meal while shooting the breeze with hosts and friends.

WINE & FARE

Silver Horse Albariño
(100% albariño)

Pair with fresh ahi poke tuna on a bed of seaweed salad.

Silver Horse Cabernet Sauvignon
(100% cabernet sauvignon)

Pair with lollipop lamb chops and baby spinach with lemon and parmigiano-reggiano salad.

Silver Horse Tempranillo
(100% tempranillo)

Pair with barbecue pizza topped with manchego cheese, chorizo sausage, arugula and yellow onions.

Silver Horse The Big Easy
(37% grenache, 33% cabernet sauvignon, 30% tempranillo)

Pair with seared, rare filet mignon bruschetta with shallots and red heirloom tomatoes.

Tastings
Open to the public, year-round

Sylvester Vineyards & Winery

Paso Robles

From a cattle ranch and hay farm to a thriving winery enterprise, Sylvester Vineyards & Winery has evolved over time, but the essence of Paso Robles runs deep through its roots. Founded in the 1960s by Austrian Sylvester Feichtinger, the established ranch became a vineyard in 1982 when the first grapes were planted. After careful propagation of imported clones and enjoying fruitful yields, Sylvester's debut wines were released in 1990. Since retiring in 2004, Sylvester's daughter Sylvia and her husband Walter Filippini run the business.

In keeping with time-honored tradition, using state-of-the-art technology along with a true passion for wine, general manager Mike Bankston was instrumental in developing Sylvester's modern winery, tasting room and gift shop. In 1995, he supervised construction of the winemaking facility with its stainless steel fermentation tanks as well as the contemporary, Austrian chalet-inspired tasting room that serves delicious paninis amid its spacious, inviting atmosphere; guests can also enjoy exquisite gourmet cheeses and chocolates perfectly paired with their reserve wines.

Sylvester's breathtaking estate vineyards are comprised of row-upon-row of varietals stemming from Bordeaux and other regions of France, and to the Tuscan hillsides of Italy that grow under the sunny skies of Paso Robles. Chardonnay, cabernet sauvignon, merlot, syrah, zinfandel, petite sirah, mourvèdre, grenache and sauvignon blanc star in Sylvester's viticultural array. Winegrapes are the most important crop, yet the Sylvester estate also grows California pistachios, organic pomegranates and olives. Above all, it is the portfolio

Top Left: Visitors are greeted by an antique wagon once used to move hay around the farm.

Middle Left: The Filippini family are proud owners of Sylvester Vineyards. Domenic, Sylvia, Kiara and Walter work together creating traditional, handcrafted wines.

Bottom Left: Upcoming vintages of Sylvester wines age peacefully in their barrel room.

Facing Page: Estate sangiovese vines, planted in 1994, soak up the Paso Robles sun.
Photographs by Maria Villano

of exceptional artisan wines crafted by winemakers Jac Jacobs and Michael Barreto that have received numerous awards, including double-gold medals for the Kiara Reserve cabernet sauvignon proudly served on luxury cruise ships like the QE2. The expressive wines are carefully crafted to be easily approachable and feature brilliant fruit aromas. The mouthfeel conveys a well-rounded richness characteristic of fine wines made in the New World style, but it is the lingering finish that gives these wines a true sense of the Paso Robles appellation.

Mike Bankston presides over the daily operations of the vineyard and winery. Seasonal social events are held outdoors on the lush 50,000-square-foot wine park property with its event center and amphitheater. Highly popular winemaker dinners are held in the park, featuring wonderful wines matched with phenomenal cuisine prepared by the winery's own classically trained Master Chef Walter Filippini. A bit of classic Americana can also be seen on the winery grounds; the founder rescued two antique Pullman sleeper railcars with one observation car and placed them in the vineyards. Tourists love the nostalgic attraction, which is open daily to the public. Private tastings are often hosted in the observation car for an extraordinary experience.

Top Left: Picturesque sunsets highlight one of the 1947 Pullman train cars at Sylvester Wine Park.
Photograph by Maria Villano

Bottom Left: The unforgettable Sylvester experience allows guests to sip wine in *The Joseph Pulitzer*, an authentic 1952 Pullman observation car.
Photograph by Maria Villano

Facing Page: Wines produced by Sylvester Winery range from rich, complex Nikiari blends to expressive and robust Le Vigne de Domenico varietals, the solid and expressive Kiara, as well as the fruit-forward and approachable Sylvester vintages.
Photograph by Mary-Ellen Felten

Sylvester wines are distributed across the nation, Southeast Asia and Europe. In addition, the Sylvester FLOCK Wine Club offers new releases mailed direct to members' doors throughout the United States, while The Cheese Society sends wine-and-cheese pairings twice a year for perfectly delectable tastings at home. The original Sylvester label depicts geese in flight to reiterate the winery's philosophy: People who share a common direction and sense of community can get where they are going with ease because they are traveling on the thrust of one another—an uplifting sentiment and all the more reason to sip and stay awhile at Sylvester Vineyards & Winery.

WINE & FARE

Kiara Reserve Chardonnay

Pair with Chaubier, a French cheese comprised of half cow's milk and half goat's milk.

Kiara Reserve Pinot Noir

Pair with Saint Agur, a triple-cream French blue cheese that hails from the Auvergne region.

Kiara Reserve Cabernet Sauvignon

Pair with Piave, an extra-aged Italian cow's milk cheese from Alto Aldige.

LeVigne di Domenico Cabernet Franc

Pair with Campo de Montalban, a Spanish cheese made of cow's, sheep's and goat's milk.

NIKIARA Meritage

(cabernet sauvignon, merlot, cabernet franc and petit verdot)

Pair with Mimolette, an extra-aged French cow's milk cheese.

Tastings

Open to the public daily, year-round

Tablas Creek Vineyard

Paso Robles

Tablas Creek Vineyard is the culmination of a decades-long friendship between two of the international wine community's leading families. Château de Beaucastel, founded in the 17th century as a retreat for the kings of France and perhaps the Rhône Valley's most renowned property, was brought to international prominence by five generations of the Perrin family. Vineyard Brands, the import company founded by Robert Haas in the 1950s, has earned a longstanding reputation as a home for wines of character and authenticity. In 1987, Robert partnered with Jean-Pierre and François Perrin to produce California's most celebrated expression of the Rhône's signature grape varieties.

Robert Haas and the Perrins spent two years searching California for the perfect spot to bring their vision to fruition. They sought high-calcium soils like those of the Rhône Valley, a long growing season perfect for late-ripening Rhône varietals, and enough rainfall to farm without annual irrigation. Two years into their quest, they found a property with rocky limestone soils nestled on the slopes of the Santa Lucia Mountains, on the western edge of the Paso Robles AVA and just 10 miles from the Pacific Ocean. They knew that Rhône varietals, especially mourvèdre and roussanne, would thrive in Paso Robles, with its Mediterranean climate of hot summer days and cold nights. They bought the 120-acre property in 1989 and named it Tablas Creek Vineyard after a small creek running through the estate. At the time, only 20 wineries were operating in the region. Now there are nearly 200 wineries in the appellation, and Paso Robles has made a sharp rise to prominence as one of the world's finest regions for Rhône grapes.

Top Left: The family-owned landmark Tablas Creek winery makes its home in Paso Robles.

Middle Left: Red wines are aged for 18 months in 1,200-gallon, authentic French oak foudres.

Bottom Left: One of the estate vineyard's ubiquitous limestone boulders has a local artist's rendering of Tablas Creek's leaf logo in copper.

Facing Page: Tablas Creek's certified organic vineyard in late spring, with cover crops still green, is reminiscent of France's picturesque Rhône Valley.
Photographs by Steve E. Miller

The partners approached the sourcing of vines for the vineyard with the same deliberation they had shown in selecting the site. Unconvinced of the quality of locally available clones, they imported select French clones from the Château de Beaucastel estate, including mourvèdre, grenache noir, syrah, roussanne, viognier and grenache blanc, and waited through a three-year USDA quarantine. The vines were released for propagation in the vineyard's on-site nursery in 1992, and the first sections of vineyard were planted in 1994. 1997 was a milestone year and included the estate's first harvest and the hiring of winemaker Neil Collins. Collins had previously worked with two pioneering Paso Robles wineries and combined extensive experience in local terroir with a like-minded winemaking philosophy—that the art of winemaking is founded on starting with the very best grapes and bringing their juice through fermentation as naturally as possible.

The team at Tablas Creek Vineyard is proud that their wines are produced exclusively from the estate vineyard. True estate wines are rare in California, but all of Tablas Creek's 16,000-case annual production is grown on the certified-organic property that surrounds the winery. Grape-growing practices are

Top Left: A flowering trellised patio outside the tasting room and winery provides an appealing alfresco lunch spot.
Photograph by Steve E. Miller

Bottom Left: One nearly ripe mourvèdre cluster glistens in the sun. Mourvèdre forms the backbone of the estate's signature Esprit de Beaucastel.
Photograph by Jason Haas, Tablas Creek Vineyard

Facing Page: The winery's collection of oak foudres allows Tablas Creek reds to soften and integrate in the manner traditional to France's Rhône Valley.
Photograph by Steve E. Miller

focused on producing a vibrantly healthy, biologically diverse vineyard, and include composting, hand-pruning, beneficial insect habitat creation and cover cropping. Winemaking techniques include hand harvesting, fermentation with native yeasts, aging in large French oak casks, and blending to produce wines that express each year's unique gifts. "We pride ourselves on not making wines that fit neatly into established categories, and we want all our wines, whether single varietals or our signature blends, to show complex flavors," emphasizes Jason Haas, Tablas Creek's general manager.

Winery visitors are treated to experiences rich in education. Seminars in which visitors can participate in the grape-growing and winemaking process are offered throughout the year, and tours of the vineyard and winery are offered daily. "We like to invite people inside the winemaking process," says Jason. The tasting room, built in 2002 and expanded in 2006, provides a space for enthusiasts to sample new releases and browse a selection of artisan gifts.

Top Left: Noticeably hilly, rugged and beautiful, the Las Tablas district is west of Paso Robles.
Photograph by Steve E. Miller

Middle Left: Wildflowers flourish in the cover crop. Cover crops retain moisture, prevent erosion, return nutrients to the soil and provide a habitat for beneficial insects.
Photograph by Steve E. Miller

Bottom Left: Syrah clusters mature during véraison in late July. Syrah provides dark color, black fruit, spice and minerals to single varietal wines and Tablas Creek's Rhône blends.
Photograph by Jason Haas, Tablas Creek Vineyard

Facing Page: Tablas Creek's signature Esprit de Beaucastel and Esprit de Beaucastel Blanc are two of California's top Rhône-style wines. Tastings also include limited-production, winery-only exclusives.
Photograph by Steve E. Miller

Tablas Creek has become one of California's most celebrated estates, with more than a dozen wines in each vintage receiving outstanding 90+ scores from Robert Parker and Stephen Tanzer, recognition as a California winery of the year from *Wine & Spirits* magazine, and features in *Wine Spectator, Saveur, Food & Wine* and *Decanter*. And yet the vineyard is remarkably unpretentious; the partners remain accessible and grounded, convinced that each vintage is a pure gift from nature and a new opportunity to produce a unique reflection of Paso Robles wine country.

Wine & Fare

Tablas Creek Esprit de Beaucastel
(mourvèdre, grenache, syrah, counoise)

Pair with game, duck, lamb or richly flavored stews.

Tablas Creek Côtes de Tablas
(grenache, syrah, mourvèdre, counoise)

Pair with grilled meats, pastas with red sauces, spicy sausages or aged hard cheeses.

Tablas Creek Rosé
(mourvèdre, grenache, counoise)

Pair with salmon, tapas, barbecue, seafood stews, and other Mediterranean fare.

Tablas Creek Esprit de Beaucastel Blanc
(roussanne, grenache blanc, picpoul blanc)

Pair with crab, lobster, grilled fish with Asian spices, and roasted or grilled vegetables.

Tastings
Open to the public daily, year-round

Talley Vineyards

Arroyo Grande

Great wines start in the vineyard. For three generations the Talley family has farmed in the Arroyo Grande Valley, located just south of San Luis Obispo in the heart of California's South Central Coast wine region. Beginning with their first vineyard plantings in 1982 and continuing today, complete control over all phases of winegrowing is the guiding principle: from the planting of vines ideally suited to each vineyard site, to viticulture and winemaking that emphasize long term sustainability, low yields and minimal processing, to the gentle bottling of the finished wine. All wines produced under the Talley Vineyards label are grown, produced and bottled by the Talley family.

The Talley family's farming legacy dates back to 1948 when Oliver Talley founded Talley Farms to grow vegetables in the Arroyo Grande Valley. Vineyards planted by Oliver's son Don Talley in 1982 and 1983 produced the first vintage of Talley Vineyards wines in 1986. Today, Talley Vineyards specializes in estate grown chardonnay and pinot noir wines from their vineyards in the Arroyo Grande Valley and Edna Valley, two neighboring AVAs ideally suited to these varietals.

High quality and long-term sustainability are the two principles that guide Talley Vineyards' farming decisions. Brian Talley and vineyard manager Kevin Wilkinson collaborate to constantly improve fruit quality while ensuring that biologically based farming techniques work in harmony with the natural conditions of the individual vineyard sites. The growing

Top Left: Rosemary's Vineyard in the Arroyo Grande Valley is well known for world-class chardonnay and pinot noir.

Bottom Left: The Talley Vineyards' tasting room welcomes guests daily.

Facing Page: Stone Corral Vineyard in beautiful Edna Valley is planted exclusively to pinot noir.
Photographs by Kirk Irwin

of premium winegrapes is labor intensive, especially the tasks of pruning, shoot thinning and canopy management. With the availability of a well-trained labor force, all of these functions are performed by hand with full-time, year-round vineyard crews. This is particularly important at harvest, the most crucial determinant of quality in the vineyard. The Talley crew mobilizes the moment the grapes reach optimum maturity, hand-harvesting during the cool early morning hours. Grapes are brought directly to the winery where they are immediately hand sorted and processed. With this hands-on involvement in every aspect of grape growing, Talley Vineyards is able to achieve superior fruit quality.

Vineyards owned and farmed by the Talley family include 28-acre Rosemary's Vineyard and 95-acre Rincon Vineyard in the Arroyo Grande Valley, where both chardonnay and pinot noir are grown. In neighboring Edna Valley, the Stone Corral Vineyard is dedicated to pinot noir, and Oliver's Vineyard specializes in chardonnay. Using fruit from these properties, Talley Vineyards seeks to create wines that reflect the unique characteristics of each vineyard.

Top Left: Talley Farm's row crops and barn are set amid the sloping hillsides of the Rincon Vineyard.

Bottom Left: Visitors can sip new releases in the tasting room while enjoying expansive vistas of vegetable fields and the Rincon Vineyard beyond.

Facing Page: The Rincon Adobe marks the entrance to Talley Vineyards and the Santa Lucia Mountains border estate vineyards to the east.
Photographs by Kirk Irwin

In the cellar, winemaker Leslie Mead employs traditional Burgundian techniques to produce expressive and complex wines. Wines are appellation-specific and often vineyard designated whether crafted under the estate grown Talley Vineyards label or the Bishop's Peak marque. Talley Vineyards is committed to the primacy of terroir in its wines, and every step taken from vine to bottle is reflective of this approach. It is this commitment that results in a consistency of quality from vintage to vintage, the hallmark of a great winegrowing estate.

The process of winemaking varies between white and red grape varieties. At Talley Vineyards, chardonnay is first cluster-sorted by hand, then whole-cluster-pressed; the juice is minimally settled in tank and then racked into French oak barrels. The wine is then barrel fermented with native yeasts and various cultured yeast strains. Talley Vineyards wines age on the lees, which are stirred weekly, and undergo malolactic fermentation to soften the natural acidity while adding richness and complexity to the finished wine. Pinot noir is predominantly destemmed after cluster sorting. Before fermentation, the must undergoes a cold soak of three to five days to extract color, aroma and flavor. Only native yeasts ferment the pinot noir, with the objective being a long, slow fermentation to maximize depth of flavor. After a cuvaison of about 10 days, the wine is racked, with minimal settling, into French oak barrels where it ages up to 18 months before bottling. Wines are gently bottled, generally without filtration.

Above: Springtime at Talley Vineyards is alive with color.

Facing Page: The Rincon Adobe, built in 1862, was the inspiration for Talley Vineyards' label design.
Photographs by Kirk Irwin

Family and farming mean everything to Brian and Johnine Talley, and their active community involvement in San Luis Obispo County is testament to the couple's genuine give-back philosophy. They established The Fund for Vineyard and Farm Workers in 2004 to assist local agricultural workers and their families in the areas of housing, healthcare and children's services. A major component of this fund is the Mano Tinta project, a charity wine produced at Talley Vineyards from donated grapes, labor and materials with all sales directly benefiting The Fund for Vineyard and Farm Workers.

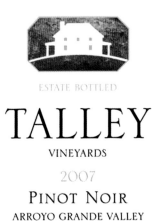

ESTATE BOTTLED

TALLEY
VINEYARDS

2007

PINOT NOIR
ARROYO GRANDE VALLEY

WINE & FARE

Rosemary's Vineyard Chardonnay, Arroyo Grande Valley
Pair with sautéed sea scallops with a saffron-lemon sauce.

Oliver's Vineyard Chardonnay, Edna Valley
Pair with halibut in a pesto-cream sauce.

Rincon Vineyard Pinot Noir, Arroyo Grande Valley
Pair with savory grilled lamb chops.

Bishop's Peak Cabernet Sauvignon
Pair with grilled steak and a wild mushroom reduction sauce.

Tastings
Open to the public daily, year-round

Treana Winery and Hope Family Wines

Paso Robles

The Hope family has been in Paso Robles since 1978. As their last name connotes, they had high expectations for the Paso Robles growing region to evolve into an important viticulture center producing world-class wines. Continuing to build on the vision of his parents—who were first orchard growers and the original winery founders—Austin Hope serves as Hope Family Wines' president and creative winemaker. He has nurtured the second-generation, family-owned estate into a prolific, well-respected California winery. Immersed in the vineyards throughout his childhood, gaining hands-on experience working with Chuck Wagner of Caymus Vineyards in his early years, earning a degree in fruit science from Cal Poly and traveling abroad, have all contributed to positioning Austin as a renowned expert in the field.

Treana Winery was established in 1996. The winery's signature moniker stems from an ancient Latin American word, *treana*, meaning a trio of natural elements combining sea, sun and soil; the acclaimed Treana Winery name captures the essence of its special Paso Robles appellation. Receiving worldwide recognition, this ideal terroir is an envied place known for its characteristic diverse soils, its proximity to the coast, and a climate of diurnal temperature shifts of up to 50 degrees, perfect for grape growing. The Treana winemaking team works closely with local farmers to get the best possible fruit from each vineyard source. The Hope Family Vineyard, nestled in the west hills of Paso Robles, stretches across 60 acres. Planted with syrah, grenache and cabernet sauvignon, it is

Top Left: Fine wine matures in imported oak barrels at the Austin Hope-Treana tasting cellar.
Photograph by Deborah Denker Photography

Bottom Left: Second-generation, visionary winemaker Austin Hope oversees the family winery.
Photograph by Katie DiSimone

Facing Page: A massive oak tree atop a hill on the Hope Family Vineyard adds character to the picturesque estate.
Photograph by Ron Bez Photography

rooted in three decades of rich history with a stellar reputation for quality, which has further defined and promoted the Paso Robles AVA internationally. Producing an abundance of varietals and artisanal wines annually, the award-winning vintners have enthusiastically distributed their well-received brands throughout the United States, Canada, Europe and the Pacific Rim.

Hope Family Wines presents four unique labels: Treana, Liberty School, Candor and Austin Hope, each with distinctive tastes based on grape varietals and specialty blends designed by artisan winemaker Austin and veteran winemakers Jason Diefenderfer and Soren Christensen. Austin's prized alternative wines bear his name and pay homage to coveted northern Rhône Valley red varieties including savory syrah as well as southern Rhône's grenache.

The Treana blends reflect Austin's philosophy that the best vineyard sites on the Central Coast, in Paso Robles and Monterey County, can hold their own with any in California; they are proprietary blends of grape

Top Left: The historic barrel room barn was converted into the winery's landmark tasting cellar.

Bottom Left: Bright and light, the tasting cellar interior surrounds guests in an atmosphere of sophistication.

Facing Page: The Austin Hope Family Wines' Treana tasting cellar boasts contemporary architecture.
Photographs by Deborah Denker Photography

varieties best suited to the climate and soils of the two regions. Treana Red gleans its flavors from the depth and power of cabernet sauvignon blended with syrah for a ripe, well-balanced luxurious wine. "We aim for wine that is not over the top, but one with grace and elegance," Austin emphasizes. It is no wonder that *Decanter* magazine's 2007 World Wine Awards named the 2003 vintage a top regional blend in North America. Inspired by wines from France's Rhône Valley, Treana White is a blend of viognier and marsanne. The resulting wine has floral aromatics, intense stone fruit flavors and overtones of honey. It possesses bright fruit to drink young, but has the right acidity and minerality to develop with age in the bottle, which is an uncommon trait for California white wines. Liberty School wines offer simple,

delicious fruit-driven, varietally correct wines enjoyed at reasonable prices. The newest label, Candor, offers blends of younger wines with older aged components to create multi-vintage wines remarkable in their complexity for even the most discerning palate, proving Austin's theory that the Old World and the New can live in harmony while truly expressing the region's vibrant fruit.

Above: A terraced vineyard east of Paso Robles yields premium grapes for Hope Family Wine's Liberty School brand.
Photograph by Bahadïr Bedenlier

Facing Page: Treana crafts elegant Rhône Valley-inspired reds and whites for sipping or pairing with gourmet fare.
Photograph by Deborah Denker Photography

The winery is open to visitors on a limited basis—its new Austin Hope-Treana tasting cellar on the Hope Family Vineyards unites with its beautiful rolling landscape accented by an impressive, old oak tree. The contemporary tasting room structure is set amid three cedar barns that house the Austin Hope Winery facility, all reflecting an understated yet grandiose style. Rustic and elegant, the Hope Family Wines landmark is worthy of note, much like its famously fine vintages.

WINE & FARE

Treana Red

Pair with grilled buffalo ribeye steak with roasted cauliflower and fiddlehead green beans.

Austin Hope Syrah

Pair with roasted filet mignon loin in a reduced wild mushroom sauce.

Austin Hope Grenache

Pair with classic favorite French coq au vin.

Treana White

Pair with seared langostinos and scallops with citrus essence or spiced lobster ceviche with ginger and coconut milk.

Tastings

Open to the public Friday and Saturday

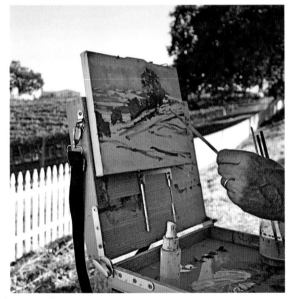

Veris Cellars

Paso Robles

W ine is a product of nature, and so it makes sense that the finest wines often come from the world's most beautiful places. The Veris Cellars estate in Paso Robles is one of these places. Here, stunning vistas and rolling vineyards are surrounded by the rugged silhouettes of coastal mountains. It is no secret why the Veris estate is the region's most photographed winery property. The beauty of this land, however, is more than cosmetic. It runs deep into the soil, into the vines, and ultimately into the wines they yield.

When Veris Cellars was founded in 1990, it was one of just 18 commercial wineries in Paso Robles, which unfolds along northern San Luis Obispo County on California's Central Coast. Today the Paso Robles appellation boasts more than 175 wineries. It is not an exaggeration to say that Veris helped establish what has since become California's most dynamic wine region.

In 2008, Veris Cellars was acquired from the original winery founders. As a local resident and wine enthusiast, acquiring the property fulfilled Matthew Talbert's long-held dream to own an estate winery on the west side of Paso Robles with a goal to nurture its time-honored tradition while taking it to the next level. The Veris Cellars estate is a special place, and Matt is dedicated to maximizing the incredible potential of its prime Central Coast terroir.

Top Left: Guests are headed directly to merlot.
Photograph by Pam Forrest

Middle Left: Natural vineyard beauty makes Veris Cellars one of the most artistically represented wineries of the Central Coast.
Photograph by Pam Forrest

Bottom Left: Acclaimed winemaker Chris Cameron welcomes visitors for a tasting.
Photograph by Ursula Cameron

Facing Page: Sunrise over the vines is an unforgettable sight.
Photograph by Pam Forrest

What sets the Veris estate apart is its remarkable combination of limestone soils, sun-kissed hillsides and refreshing ocean breezes that cascade through the Templeton Gap, a notch in the coastal mountains. Limestone soils are recognized as a distinguishing factor in many of the world's finest wines, and they are similarly responsible for the distinctive character of Veris wines. Veris vineyards are known for growing merlot, zinfandel, cabernet sauvignon, syrah, sangiovese, petit syrah, petite verdot, cabernet franc,

Above: Nothing compares to sitting outside on a warm summer's eve sipping a glass of sauvignon blanc.
Photograph by Ursula Cameron

Left: Another glowing sunset on the Victorian tasting room marks the end of a fulfilling day.
Photograph by Chris Cameron

Facing Page Top: Owner-proprietor Matthew Talbert lives his dream in the Paso Robles appellation.
Photograph by Pam Forrest

Facing Page Bottom: Spring truly begins in the estate vineyard with a profusion of flowers.
Photograph by Ursula Cameron

mourvèdre, chardonnay and viognier. The established label is celebrated for its mastery of unique blends such as the Picaro, Riatta and Crossfire, a signature blend of cabernet, merlot and syrah. Deemed as decidedly fruit-forward, Veris wines exemplify the result of handcrafted expertise from planting and grafting to growing and artfully bottling each single varietal or creative blend.

Internationally applauded winemaker Chris Cameron has a committed and passionate approach to all aspects of winemaking, with minimalist intervention at the core of his philosophy. He feels that truly great wines are dependent on fruit quality and the art is the ability to translate what is grown on the vine to the bottle. Chris's interpretations have heralded a new era for the winery and are an accurate reflection of varietals grown in the Paso Robles appellation.

The boutique winery welcomes visitors daily to its charming tasting room, which occupies a historic Victorian home built in 1892, completely restored in 1990. Newly planted gardens unfold in waves of color across the property, while two spacious patios and an arbor showcase the estate's breathtaking vineyard views. Veris Cellars has undeniably evolved into a premier Paso Robles' wine tasting destination.

Above: Sun-kissed grapes announce harvest time in the vineyard.

Facing Page: Veris Cellars' 2005 vintage wines age gracefully.
Photographs by Pam Forrest

For Matt and his vintner team, the most gratifying part of the winery experience is personally sharing their award-winning wines with all who visit and imparting the winery's friendly philosophy— each handcrafted wine is a timeless treasure best enjoyed amongst family and friends. A warmhearted welcome and vast wine selection awaits guests, with a personal toast to the abundant fruit of the vines from the man with a passion for the land.

WINE & FARE

JanKris Sauvignon Blanc
(100% sauvignon blanc)

Pair with prawn and chicken wonton soup.

JanKris Divinity
(60% chardonnay, 40% sauvignon blanc)

Pair with coconut shrimp skewers with wombok salad.

JanKris Crossfire
(50% cabernet sauvignon, 25% merlot, 25% syrah)

Pair with mustard lamb cutlets with mint aioli and char-grilled potatoes.

JanKris Syrah
(100% syrah)

Pair with peppered beef, almond and broccolini stir-fry.

Tastings
Open to the public daily, year-round

Vina Robles Winery

Paso Robles

The Gold Rush era attracted prospectors from around the world to seek good fortune in a state known for its bounty of resources. Swiss-born Hans Nef is a different kind of prospector; a modern-day discoverer arriving more than a century later. In 1996, he found the perfect parcels of agricultural land on which to build his vision. With his Swiss-lineage, he developed vineyards and a brand on American terroir—the equivalent of France's Bordeaux and Rhône Valley wine country—smack-dab in the middle of California's Central Coast.

Hans partnered with colleague Hans R. Michel to build his dream, joining with acclaimed winemaker Matthias Gubler to produce their first vintage in 1999. Since their collaboration, the vignerons have created some of the most outstanding wines stemming from the Central Coast. The founders quickly ascertained that Paso Robles was a place to grow pure varietals on eclectic vineyard blocks, which now produce more than 20 types of grapes. The winery's motto, "European Inspiration—California Character," speaks to the partners' appreciation for this world-class AVA. Grapes are sourced from four estate vineyards: Huerhuero and Creston Vineyards situated on sandy hillsides, Jardine Vineyard poised on flatland and Pleasant Valley Vineyard set in Paso Robles' north corner. The ancient seabed soil is the real secret to premium grape production with its ideal sandy loam, mixed clay and limestone. From grape to glass, Matthias has crafted award-winning vintages with Syrée winning "Best Rhône Blend of California," and Suendero, a classic Meritage earning "Best of Show" at the Houston Livestock Show & Rodeo International Wine Competition. Reminiscent of authentic European vintages, wine profiles express a respect for the vibrant fruit of the vine: bright and clean with an elegant finish. Guests can enjoy a taste in the Mission-style tasting room or host a social event in the airy Signature Room while drinking in new releases and the oak-studded vineyard view.

Top Left: Evening at the Vina Robles Hospitality Center promises fine wines and conviviality.

Middle Left: Vina Robles's elegant tasting room ambience invites all to discover new vintages.

Bottom Left: The European bistro-style Petite Terrace is ideal for picnicking and relaxing alfresco with your favorite Vina Robles wine.

Facing Page: Refreshing fountain sounds welcome winery guests at the picture-perfect Jardine Court.
Photographs courtesy of Vina Robles Winery

Windward Vineyard

Paso Robles

Raise a glass of what may be the greatest American pinot noir, affectionately known as "the noble juice." Here's a toast to winemaker extraordinaire Marc Goldberg and Maggie D'Ambrosia, the husband-wife team of Windward Vineyard. The story began many years ago, when Marc swept Maggie off her feet with a bottle of Domaine de la Romanée-Conti 1959. They soon married and had thriving careers as hospital executives in cities across the United States. Marc's longtime dream of having a winery after retirement was realized in the west side of the beautiful Paso Robles appellation, where they discovered the ideal terroir and made their home.

Windward Vineyard's name says it all. In 1989, Marc and Maggie acquired 26 prime acres on the west side of Paso Robles, in the Templeton Gap tucked at the center of the Santa Lucia Mountain chain with its unique calcareous soils and microclimate, cooled by brisk breezes from the Pacific. This was the ideal place to nurture their vines: 100-percent estate-grown pinot noir. Marc and Maggie passionately produce handcrafted Burgundian-style pinot noir. With over 1,500 years of development in French Burgundy and a favorite of Napoleon Bonaparte, the history and quality of classic Burgundian wines fascinated Marc. He modeled his vineyard and winery after the great French winemaking tradition, planting 15 precious acres in 1990. Inspired by famed vigneron Dr. Stanley Hoffman from HMR and enologist André Tchelistcheff, Marc and other area pioneers became winemaker friends on a mission. They brought notable French clones to California and collaboratively produced the first Windward Cuvée 1990, which marked the beginning of the Central Coast rise to popularity. The small-lot Windward winery was built in 1993 and

Top Left: The Windward Vineyard tasting room welcomes guests to sample a vertical of award-winning estate pinot noir wines.

Bottom Left: Co-owners Maggie D'Ambrosia and Marc Goldberg live on the vineyard property and love to share a sip of "the noble juice" with visitors.

Facing Page: The winery's more than one hundred-year-old cellar stores precious vintages from the 1990 Windward prototype to collectible large format bottles.
Photographs by Maria Villano

produces at most 2,000 cases per year, wines that are sold out upon release. Windward's award-winning wines have earned gold medals, and a recent vintage has been dubbed the "Most Burgundian of American Pinot Noir." Perhaps it is the land, its fruit and the way in which wines are gently handcrafted and finished in subtly scented Bourgogne Grand Cru French oak barrels that has wine club members ordering new releases the moment they emerge.

Pinot noir loves calcareous soils and Windward Vineyard's 1,100-foot elevation and soil structure is similar to the revered Burgundy region of France. Marc planted his first cuttings when there were only 16 wineries in existence, yet hundreds of winegrape growers already understood the benefits of the region's ancient land: a 45-million-year-old alluvial plane pushed up from a continental plate, which was once under the ocean. The owners made an amazing discovery on their property; they unearthed vertebrae bones from a 25-foot-long whale that archeologists believe to be 10 million years old.

Left: A vintage barn houses the Old World-style tasting room featuring colorful artwork created by local talent.
Top photograph courtesy of Windward Vineyard
Bottom photograph by Maria Villano

Facing Page: Unique 15th harvest 2007 Windward Vineyard Monopole GOLD Barrel Select and 2007 Windward Vineyard Monopole pinot noirs delight connoisseurs and newcomers alike. Bacchus, the Roman god of wine, adorns every label.
Photograph by Maria Villano

The couple works the land and runs the winery, involved in every aspect of the operation from overseeing viticulture to handcrafting the artisan wines. Living on the premises with their son Justin, Maggie and Marc enjoy relaxing on the patio, gazing at the expansive vineyard view and feeling the maritime winds as they cool the grapes. A traditional vigneron, Marc deems himself the "wine shepherd" of Paso Robles. He is a minimalist, assuring that the vibrant fruit makes it into each bottle with little handling and zero filtering. Indeed, discerning drinkers are drawn to the finesse and elegance captured in every drop.

WINE & FARE

Windward Monopole Pinot Noir
(100% estate pinot noir)

Pair with lamb or duck dishes and imported cheeses like Taleggio, pecorino tartufo, Manchego, Tomme de Savoie and Époisses de Bourgogne.

Windward Gold Barrel Select Monopole Pinot Noir
(100% estate pinot noir)

Pair with grilled salmon, wild game or duck confit.

Tastings
Open to the public daily, year-round

Talbott Vineyards, page 144

Hahn Family Wines, page 134

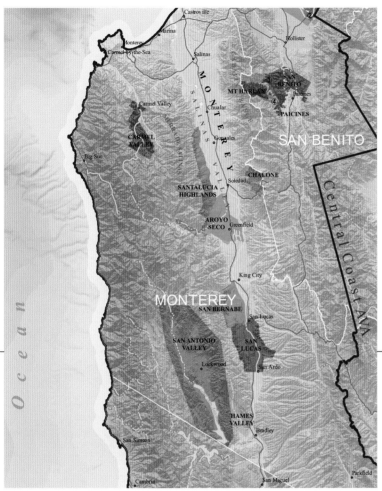

Ocean

Castroville
Marina
Monterey
Carmel-by-the-Sea
Salinas

Carmel Valley

CARMEL
VALLEY

Big Sur

SANTA LUCIA
HIGHLANDS

AROYO
SECO

MONTEREY

SAN BERNABE

SAN ANTONIO
VALLEY

Lockwood

San Simeon

HAMES
VALLEY

Cambria

San Miguel

Hollister

MT HARLAN

SAN
BENITO

Paicines

PAICINES

SAN BENITO

CHALONE
Soledad

Greenfield

King City

San Lucas

SAN
LUCAS
San Ardo

Bradley

Parkfield

Chualar

Gonzales

MONTEREY

SALINAS VALLEY

Central Coast AVA

Map provided by www.vestra.com

Monterey
County

Chalone Vineyard

Soledad

I f ever a sense of place played an important role in winemaking heritage it is at Chalone Vineyard.® Chalone Vineyard stands out as being synonymous with the land it encompasses. The property was discovered in 1969 by founder-visionary Dick Graff, who advocated estate wineries and traditional European methods and worked to produce some of the region's top dry white wines. Chalone Vineyard built its winery in 1972 on this virtually untouched land rich with history and rugged beauty, surrounded by spectacular flora and fauna, and marked by the Pinnacles National Monument amid remnants of an ancient volcano.

The Chalone American Viticultural Area moniker, like that of the winery, comes from the name of a group of Native Americans who once inhabited the area. Its fertile limestone soils were rediscovered by founding viticulturists to be the ideal terroir for abundant grape-growing, particularly for the chardonnay and pinot noir varietals. Chalone Vineyard chardonnay has been considered a benchmark for California chardonnays for more than 40 years, and its pinot noirs were hailed as the landmark California version of Burgundian pinot noirs. In 1976, when a number of California wines were pitted against their French counterparts, the Chalone Vineyard chardonnay proved that it could hold its own next to the best from Europe. Today Chalone Vineyard is owned by Diageo Chateau & Estate Wines.

Top Left: The vineyard sits at an elevation of 1,700 feet with views of Mount Chalone in the distance.

Bottom Left: Craggy spires of Pinnacles National Monument form a dramatic backdrop for the vineyard.

Facing Page: The Chalone Vineyard label was inspired by Pinnacles National Monument, visible from several blocks on the vineyard property.
Photographs by R. Valentine Atkinson

Wines displaying the Chalone Vineyard Estate Grown label are produced from the remote estate vineyard, which sits at an elevation of 1,700 feet and has vines dating back to the early 1900s. The area's daytime climate is slightly warmer than that of the Salinas Valley floor, ensuring that grapes achieve full ripeness. At night, the temperature drops about 40 degrees, giving the grapes ideal acidity. The region's characteristic granite and limestone soils are very well drained and therefore naturally limit vine vigor. This low yield is the secret to intensely flavored yet balanced wines, renowned for complexity and aging potential. Chalone's award-winning white wines are valued for their minerality, which gives them a subtle, structured character. Chardonnay, pinot noir, pinot blanc, chenin blanc and syrah are the leading varietals crafted by seasoned vintner Robert Cook, who pays painstaking attention to detail and possesses a patient nature. "Fine winemaking is all about patience," emphasizes Robert.

The picturesque Salinas Valley and Gavilan Mountains are home to the 1,000-acre Chalone Vineyard. This breathtaking region of Monterey County has been the source of inspiration not only for winemaking pioneers but for modern-day enologists as well. Even the Chalone Vineyard label, which bears a stunning

Top Left: Natural underground caves provide ideal temperatures and humidity for aging Chalone Vineyard wines.

Middle Left: The sun-drenched outcroppings are remnants of an ancient volcano and reflect the ruggedness of this land.

Bottom Left: Standing in solitude, Chalone Vineyard is the only winery that can claim the Chalone appellation as its home.

Facing Page: Limited rainfall and high altitude stresses the vines, producing concentrated, robust wines.
Photographs by R. Valentine Atkinson

silhouette of the Pinnacles National Monument, pays homage to the rare landscape. Perhaps the best illustration is Nobel Prize-winning novelist John Steinbeck's vivid description of the valley and mountains. He painted a picture from memory in such detail that readers were transported to this compelling land, much like those who have tasted the majestic sense of place infused throughout Chalone Vineyard wines.

CHALONE VINEYARD.®

WINE & FARE

Chalone Vineyard Chardonnay

Pair with rich, robust dishes such as pasta in cream sauce, poached salmon and roasted chicken.

Chalone Vineyard Pinot Noir

Pair with roasted turkey, seared duck with cherry sauce, grilled salmon and wild mushroom risotto.

Chalone Vineyard Syrah

Pair with seared duck breast, peppery beef daube or herb-crusted rack of lamb.

Chalone Vineyard Pinot Blanc

Pair with Asian fusion dishes, spiced pork chops and fresh seafood.

Tastings
*Open by appointment only Monday through Friday
Open to the public Saturday and Sunday*

Hahn Family Wines

Santa Lucia Highlands, Monterey County

There is something to crow about at Hahn Family Wines. The winery was founded by Nicolaus Hahn as Smith & Hook in 1980 when he purchased two hillside vineyards in Monterey County belonging to the Smith and Hook families. These first vineyards took root in 1974 marked by a debut cabernet sauvignon; the pure varietal was quickly discovered and highly ranked by Robert Parker. This 1985 vintage cabernet became a star on the Monterey County map at a time when the Santa Lucia Highlands appellation was emerging as a recognized grape-growing region. Today the appellation is known for its incomparable Burgundian topography and mountain-air climate.

Nicky envisioned greatness in the 1980s when only a half dozen vineyards dotted the hills; he was instrumental in defining this relatively small but exciting SLH appellation of the California Central Coast as a world-class winemaking region. In 1991, after acquiring more vineyards and several harvests later, Nicky began what is known as Hahn Estates, a moniker for his beloved family-owned, 936-acre vineyard. The family's Swiss heritage shed light on the name "Hahn." Derived from the German language, the name means rooster, which inspired the classic red rooster symbol as the brand's plucky identity.

The rugged Santa Lucia Highlands overlooks the Salinas Valley in the Monterey appellation where Hahn Family Wines makes its home. Multiple vineyards cover the rolling acreage of the picturesque estate that proudly produces 400,000 cases of award-winning wines annually. Pinot noir, pinot gris, syrah and chardonnay are the vintners' premier grapes,

Top Left: With its carved red rooster emblem, the Hahn Estates entrance is impressively marked.

Bottom Left: The Hahn Family Wines vintners, Gaby and Nicolaus Hahn, enjoy a glass of their prized pinot noir.

Facing Page: Hahn Estates vineyards, nestled in the highly regarded Santa Lucia Highlands appellation, overlook the fertile Salinas Valley.
Photographs by Maria Villano

abundantly grown on six scenic vineyards: Lone Oak Vineyard, Smith & Hook, St. Philippe, Doctor's and St. Nicholas Vineyards. The coveted terroir boasts four distinctive grapes and has inspired the winery's well-established labels: Hahn Estates Winery, Smith & Hook, Hahn SLH Estate and the prestigious Lucienne.

The owners have received numerous accolades including gold medals that designate Hahn as the United States leader for two consecutive years, thanks in great measure to the expert winemaking of Paul Clifton. Paul is the winery's head winemaker—a homegrown vintner raised in Salinas—who earned his master's degree in viticulture while attending university in New Zealand. He gained much of his winemaking experience working for several Central Coast wineries prior to joining Hahn Family Wines.

His series of balanced, handcrafted vintages are distributed in all 50 states and 30 countries worldwide, from ever-popular, affordable bottlings to the refined, Lucienne pinot noir limited edition.

Originally horse and cattle ranch land, the destination winery sits amid the wide-open spaces of the Santa Lucia Mountain range. Hahn Family Wines is one of Monterey County's largest producing establishments with its official tasting room attracting up to 14,000 wine-loving visitors every year. Guests can enjoy sampling great wines while learning about viticulture

Above: The lawn is surrounded by picturesque family-owned vineyards, making it a popular spot for parties, picnics and wedding celebrations.

Right: Hahn Estates is known for growing world-class quality winegrapes in the Santa Lucia Highlands.

Facing Page: Visitors are warmly welcomed to the Hahn Estates tasting room, where sampling a wide selection of wines is encouraged.
Photographs by Maria Villano

practices in the adjacent demonstration vineyard. The tasting room is perched on a 1,000-foot elevation point with spectacular panoramic views that can also be savored from the picnic grounds or hiking trails; guests clearly see the ancient volcano at Pinnacles National Monument while sipping some of the region's prized pinot noir. But it is the warm hospitality of the winery that brings people back again and again. The landmark winery is a popular place for wedding ceremonies and special events year-round on the lawn with its breathtaking vineyard and valley backdrops.

A firm commitment to sustainable farming methods makes Hahn Family Wines a credit to California's Central Coast. The owners have worked hard to earn the winery's certified sustainable status, a testament to being good stewards of the earth through sustainable growing and recycling practices. Always innovative, the Hahn Estate stays in tune with market trends and is truly devoted to quality. "It is incumbent on us to be a leader in the Central Coast," affirms winery president Bill Leigon.

Top Left: The charming Hahn Estates tasting room promises a relaxing place to sip wine and converse.

Middle Left: Visitors of Hahn Estates can savor expansive vistas and breathtaking views from the patio.

Bottom Left: The Hahn Estates tasting room offers wine samples, wine club opportunities and a tasteful selection of gifts, as well as original artwork created by Gaby Hahn.

Facing Page: Hahn SLH and Hahn Estates wine bottles proudly display their signature red rooster labels.
Photographs by Maria Villano

The Hahn family has pioneered California's winemaking industry but has expanded their sphere of influence to support performing arts programs as well as to cultivate global philanthropy. Nicky and his artist-wife Gaby are passionate about preserving wildlife on their 49,000-acre Mutamaiyu Mugie Ranch in Kenya, while also providing a top-rated school for the working ranch hands' children. Conservationists and visionaries, the Hahns work with a spirit of enthusiasm to benefit others, just as they do in their renowned winemaking tradition.

WINE & FARE

Hahn SLH 2007 Pinot Gris

Pair with oysters or clams steamed on the grill in butter, scallions, fresh salt and a splash of pinot gris alongside grilled corn on the cob.

Hahn SLH 2006 Chardonnay

Serve with chicken baked in a mushroom and shallot reduction over Asiago-topped wild mushroom risotto.

Hahn SLH 2006 Pinot Noir

Pair with vinaigrette-glazed grilled ahi with spinach and mixed green salad in a raspberry vinaigrette with berries, red onions, avocado and goat cheese.

Hahn SLH 2007 Syrah

Pair with sage-butter glazed grilled pork loin filled with a spinach and white onion ragout. Finish with a fresh fruit cobbler.

Tastings
Open to the public daily, year-round

Paraiso Vineyards

Soledad

Paraiso Vineyards lies on what is indeed the epitome of wine country with its awe-inspiring beauty and heritage of hard-working California farmers. Life in the fertile Salinas Valley is rich with nature's gifts, and so the winery's name "paraiso" is quite fitting—it is the Spanish word for paradise. Paraiso Vineyards' terroir possesses visually stunning topography of rolling hills, canyons and peaks with rare microclimates—due to varying 400- to 800-foot elevations—and complex soils, all beneficial to exceptional grape-growing.

Rich and Claudia Smith discovered their piece of viticultural paradise in the early 1970s, long before most vineyards and wineries popped up along the Salinas River. Considered the first family of winemaking in the Santa Lucia Highlands, the Smiths ventured together with a handful of other passionate pioneers into the grape-growing business. The original founders virtually wrote the book on growing vinifera in Monterey County and also helped to outline and establish its world-class Santa Lucia Highlands appellation. Today a second Smith generation has inherited the same love for the land and continues to grow wine-worthy fruit on 3,000 acres of vineyards, providing grapes of stature to 25 well-known wine producers. The family-owned growers have earned SIP™ certification, for their sustainable farming practices and dedication to being diligent stewards of the land, always mindful of future generations.

Top Left: Paraiso Vineyards is situated on the southern end of the Santa Lucia Highlands appellation in Monterey County.
Photograph by Maria Villano

Bottom Left: A romantic terrace behind the tasting room offers sweeping views of vineyards and the Salinas Valley.
Photograph by Peter Malinowski

Facing Page: Paraiso's chardonnay and pinot noir vines grow at elevations of 400 to 800 feet.
Photograph courtesy of Paraiso Vineyards

In 2005, the Paraiso Vineyards estate winery came to fruition; the founding vintners' son and general manager Jason Smith partnered with winemaker David Fleming to craft fine wines from 250 acres of select estate-grown varietals, mainly classic chardonnay and pinot noir. This family-owned winery prides itself on creating cool-climate estate varietals assigned to designated blocks, focusing on their Burgundian-style wines derived from estate chardonnay and pinot noir as well as riesling, a bit of syrah and souzao port. "The backbone of our wines are our old grapevines that were my parents' original plantings from 1973," emphasizes Jason," but with a mix of new clones for innovative winemaking options." Premium fruit is harvested and delivered to the winery each vintage, where it is aged in French oak barrels. "I am continually inspired to make wines that best express the unique terroir of the Santa Lucia Highlands," says winemaker David, who hails from UC Davis. Paraiso's 2007 estate vintages have garnered prestigious rankings from *Wine Advocate* and *Wine Spectator,* and more accolades steadily pour in from other well-respected wine experts.

Awards aside, an authentic sense of family and a sense of place reign supreme at Paraiso Vineyards. Co-owner and Jason's wife Jennifer Smith extends genuine hospitality to visitors in the tasting room, while loyal wine club members have the opportunity

Top Left: Meet the heart and soul of Paraiso Vineyards: winemaker Dave Fleming, general manager Jason Smith and hospitality director Jennifer Murphy-Smith.
Photograph by Peter Malinowski

Middle Left: In addition to delicious Paraiso wines, the sunny tasting room features a chic home décor and gift boutique.
Photograph by Peter Malinowski

Bottom Left: Second and third generations of the Smith family share their passion with key members of the Paraiso winemaking team.
Photograph by Peter Malinowski

Facing Page: The family's longstanding love for the land and its abundant fruit inspires each and every vintage.
Photograph courtesy of Paraiso Vineyards

to experience the estate's new releases by mail. Locals and visitors are invited to enjoy Paraiso's approachable, handcrafted wines in the vineyard setting for a true taste of the mighty grape. The Smith family loves being an integral part of the revered grape-growing AVA, uniting neighbors and friends with their lifelong passion.

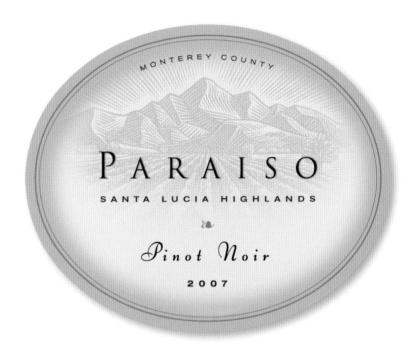

Wine & Fare

Paraiso Estate Chardonnay

Pair with simple Alfredo pasta, rosemary-lemon chicken or a romantic comedy and lightly salted popcorn.

Paraiso Estate Pinot Noir

Pair with pesto pasta with sundried tomatoes, garlic-roasted pork loin or an action film with hot dogs and chips.

Paraiso Estate Riesling

Pair with cheese-filled jalapenos, traditional chile rellenos, take-out Thai food with spicy curry or a drama flick with hot tamales.

Paraiso Estate Syrah

Pair with traditional lasagne, spaghetti and meatballs, grilled T-bone steak or a good suspense movie with pepperoni pizza.

Tastings
Open to the public daily, year-round

Talbott Vineyards

Santa Lucia Highlands • Carmel Valley

In 1982, Robert Talbott began planting his original Diamond T Estate vineyard on a cold, windswept mountaintop in Carmel Valley. Conventional wisdom was against him, and many said the steep, exposed site with its massive shale boulders was too cold, too difficult to plant and much too challenging to grow on. But Robb had a vision—a vision he held on to as he prepared the cliffside vineyard by hand, breaking apart its massive boulders with a 12-pound sledgehammer. "It all began with my first taste of a great Burgundy," says Robb. That experience profoundly shaped his palate, and as he grew older Robb knew that he wanted to create unique and exceptional chardonnays and pinot noirs. He dreamt of making wines inspired by the tradition of Burgundy, but with their roots in California's unique soils.

To achieve this goal, Robb Talbott established one of the Central Coast's most esteemed estate programs featuring two of Monterey County's grand cru sites: Diamond T Estate and the legendary Sleepy Hollow Vineyard in the Santa Lucia Highlands. Though located a mere 18 miles apart, these two vineyards offer remarkably different growing conditions, yielding rich and distinctive chardonnays and pinot noirs that embody their unique terroirs.

At its heart, the history of Talbott Vineyards is the story of one family's determined focus and commitment to excellence. In 1950, Robert Talbott Sr., his wife Audrey and their son Robb moved to Carmel, California, where they started a luxury tie company. Audrey sewed the ties by hand and Robert Sr. sold them up and down the California

Top Left: Founder Robb Talbott and winemaker Dan Karlsen at Talbott's acclaimed Sleepy Hollow Vineyard, framed by the Santa Lucia Mountains.

Middle Left: Pinot noir grapes change color in the process of véraison at Sleepy Hollow Vineyard.

Bottom Left: Original chardonnay plantings from 1982 grow in the thin, chalky-shale soils of Talbott's mountaintop Diamond T Estate.

Facing Page: Chardonnay vines on the steep slopes of Diamond T Estate bask in the sun. Amid Carmel Valley, this picturesque vineyard benefits from cooling marine influences.
Photographs by Marc Cutino

coast. During silk-buying business trips to Europe, the Talbotts often visited French and Italian vineyards and soon became interested in the art of fine wine. As their interests grew, they aspired to produce their own California wines using the Burgundian techniques that they had become passionate about.

In 1982, Robb planted Diamond T and simultaneously built the original winery in idyllic Carmel Valley. For his first plantings, Robb selected the storied Corton-Charlemagne chardonnay clone, planting it in Diamond T's almost soil-free, chalky shale. Robb knew that the vines would have to struggle to survive at Diamond T, producing miniscule yields that always create wines of great intensity.

After years of working with fruit harvested from Sleepy Hollow Vineyard, the Talbotts achieved another important milestone when they were able to acquire the prime property in 1994, making Talbott an all-estate winery. Featuring blocks of old Wente clone vines planted in 1972, Sleepy Hollow has earned a reputation for producing wines of great depth and voluptuousness. In fact, the 1990 vintage of Talbott's flagship Sleepy Hollow Vineyard Chardonnay received an exceedingly rare, perfect score of 100 points in a blind taste test by *Wine Spectator* magazine.

Above: The idyllic Talbott Vineyards tasting room in Carmel Valley is a mecca for lovers of cool-climate chardonnay and pinot noir wines.

Facing Page: Freshly harvested pinot grapes from Diamond T Estate rest in the shade while awaiting first crush.
Photographs by Marc Cutino

Today, Sleepy Hollow's River Road block is home to the winery's state-of-the-art winemaking facility where Robb and renowned winemaker Dan Karlsen guide Talbott's storied chardonnay and pinot noir programs. These premium estate wines have gained a reputation for their lushness, grace and great aging potential, and have become benchmarks of quality on the Central Coast.

WINE & FARE

Talbott Sleepy Hollow Vineyard Chardonnay

Pair with seafood and rich fish such as salmon, swordfish or monkfish.

Talbott Diamond T Estate Chardonnay

Pair with grilled lobster, Alaskan king crab legs or fresh oysters.

Talbott Sleepy Hollow Vineyard Pinot Noir

Pair with wild salmon or herb-crusted rack of lamb.

Talbott Cuvée RFT Diamond T Pinot Noir

Pair with duck breast in a tart cherry sauce.

Tastings
Open to the public daily, year-round

Bridlewood Estate Winery, page 154

Zaca Mesa Winery & Vineyards, page 166

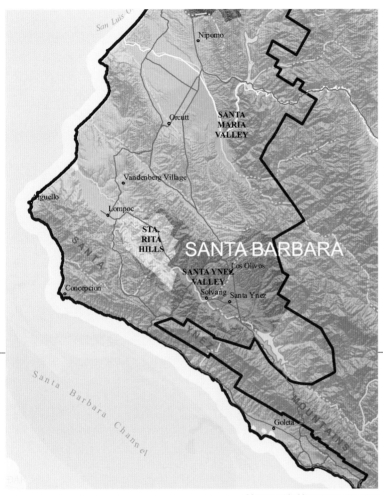

Nipomo

Orcutt

SANTA MARIA VALLEY

Vandenberg Village

Arguello

Lompoc

STA. RITA HILLS

SANTA BARBARA

S A N T A

SANTA YNEZ VALLEY

Los Olivos

Concepcion

Solvang   Santa Ynez

San Luis O.

Santa Barbara Channel

Y N E Z

MOUNTAINS

Goleta

Map provided by www.vestra.com

Santa Barbara
County

Alma Rosa Winery & Vineyards

Buellton

Ever notice the first wine tasting room featured in the independent film "Sideways"? Step into Alma Rosa Winery & Vineyards for a look at what winemaking should be: nature and agriculture in sustainable harmony. Richard Sanford came to the Santa Ynez Valley in 1970 after recognizing the potential of the Santa Rita Hills, which is now an officially accredited American Viticultural Area. A pioneer in winemaking, he was first to plant pinot noir vines on the region's renowned terroir.

Richard and Thekla Sanford, who have farmed their vineyards organically for over 20 years, are veteran growers and vintners with a sustainable winemaking history. Inspired by the Burgundy region, Richard had a dream to create wines that rival the finest of France. But it was his joint vision with wife Thekla that led to becoming the original certified organic vineyard in the Santa Rita Hills AVA. Richard's winemaking and viticulture inspiration is derived from the French, but his knowing comes from within; he clearly distinguishes between organic-sustainable and conventional agriculture. Once a traditional farmer using toxic pesticides, Richard began to think about harmful effects on water resources and investigated the old farming practices that were in place before chemicals became available. With Thekla's encouragement, he weaned the vineyard off of all chemicals in 1985. Working in partnership with a reverence for nature, the Sanfords founded multiple, successful winegrowing enterprises.

Top Left: The entrance sign at Alma Rosa Winery & Vineyards welcomes guests to the iconic tasting room at Rancho El Jabali, first stop in the movie "Sideways."

Middle Left: Natural gravity-flow springs provide water for the fountains at the tasting complex, adding charming serenity to the rustic, creekside setting.

Bottom Left: Visitors are encouraged to linger on the tasting room patio, enjoying the flower-filled gardens and shade of the ramada.

Facing Page: A springtime view from La Encantada Vineyard looks west across the Santa Ynez River Valley into the Santa Rita Hills; the Pacific Ocean is only 20 miles away.
Photographs by Peter Malinowski

Today Alma Rosa Winery & Vineyards represents the culmination of a lifetime's experience. It is a family-owned business dedicated to creating high quality wines while setting a benchmark for organic farming, sustainable agricultural methods and environmentally friendly commerce. Visionary idealism coupled with UC Berkeley geography studies have helped Richard to understand the regional growing climate with its east-west valleys and maritime influences; he farms in unison with nature's gifts cultivating a spiritual Taoist philosophy along the way.

Connecting to the earth and nature, Richard and Thekla nurture more than 100 acres of pinot noir and chardonnay, as well as pinot gris and pinot blanc. Their three-fold mantra is to enjoy good food, good wine and a sustainable future. A deep and long-standing commitment to the environment sets this winery and its vineyards apart. Burgundian Christian Roguenant is head winemaker and brings seasoned experience to the table; he is known for handcrafting pure varietal expressions of award-winning quality. All of Alma Rosa's wines are tank-fermented or aged in French oak, creating well-balanced vintages. Bottles are sealed without conventional corks using twist-off caps instead, a responsible packaging idea to ensure the mustiness of cork taint does not spoil the wines.

Top Left: The tasting room and offices of Alma Rosa Winery & Vineyards are in converted barns and sustainably built structures made entirely from recycled materials.

Bottom Left & Facing Page: Visitors are welcome to peruse the Sanfords' personal wine reference library in the tasting room.
Photographs by Peter Malinowski

"Richard and I share in a commitment of integrity toward environmental responsibility, viticultural practices and the sustainable conduct of our business. We are here to support the natural resources given to us," says Thekla. Ethics and excellence go hand in hand at historic Alma Rosa; grapes grown and wines made on the couples' beloved 110 acres reflect the essence of the land, the soul of Rancho Santa Rosa.

WINE & FARE

2007 Pinot Gris, La Encantada Vineyard
(100% pinot gris)

Pair with spicy Asian-inspired dishes, robust Mediterranean vegetables and seafood or East-Indian cuisine.

2006 Pinot Blanc, La Encantada Vineyard
(100% pinot blanc)

Pair with fresh shellfish, crab cakes, roasted vegetables, seafood pasta or roasted herb chicken.

2006 Chardonnay, El Jabalí Vineyard
(100% chardonnay)

Pair with stir-fry dishes, roasted fish with fruit salsa, herbed grilled chicken, crispy fried trout or Southern fried chicken.

2006 Pinot Noir, La Encantada Vineyard
(100% pinot noir)

Pair with grilled or roasted game, mushroom and Tasso pasta, paprika-rubbed pork ribs or lamb chops.

Tastings
Open to the public daily, year-round

Bridlewood Estate Winery

Santa Barbara County

Epitomizing the Central Coast's burgeoning reputation as a premier wine-growing region, Bridlewood Estate Winery has become one of Santa Barbara wine country's most sought-after artisan brands. A glimpse of the winery's charming historic property—complete with mission-style architecture and working bells—beckons visitors to discover the winery's exceptional vintages and embrace the spirit of this very special place.

Established in 1999 amid quintessential Santa Barbara ranch country, the estate was initially part of the Santa Ynez Mission founded by the Franciscan brotherhood in Santa Barbara province; the original mission land grant extends throughout Bridlewood's landscaped hillside vineyards. The winery's rich history is evidenced by 18th-century architectural roots making it an iconic landmark in the region; its traditional Spanish Mission-style structure is topped by an authentic terracotta tile roof and triple mission bell façade, underscored by a sun-drenched courtyard with welcoming fountains.

Bridlewood's staple varietal stems from the notable block of land that is home to 40-acres of estate grown syrah. But it is the Central Coast's microclimate and exceptional soil that contribute to the tremendous diversity and flavors of wines crafted at Bridlewood. Acclaimed winemaker David Hopkins is renowned for crafting wines that showcase

Top Left: The 105-acre Bridlewood Estate Winery sits on an ancient seabed in the Santa Ynez Valley at the heart of California's Central Coast winegrowing region.
Photograph courtesy of Bridlewood Estate Winery

Middle Left: A self-proclaimed "flavor guy," winemaker David Hopkins artfully blends fruit from multiple vineyards creating wines that reflect the diversity of the Central Coast growing region.
Photograph courtesy of Bridlewood Estate Winery

Bottom Left: Bridlewood's charming central courtyard, with its adobe tile roof and hacienda-style hallways, is reminiscent of the nearby Santa Ynez Mission.
Photograph courtesy of Bridlewood Estate Winery

Facing Page: The towering winery façade features iconic functioning mission-style bells that pay tribute to the inspired history of the region.
Photograph by Peter Malinowski

California's finest grapes. He is most recognized for the special care he brings in his approach to blending wines for character and balance, achieving award-winning marks from wine critics both at home and abroad. The winemaker has masterfully captured the rich range of flavors derived from the vineyards throughout the Central Coast, creating sophisticated yet approachable wines. "I'm a passionate flavor guy, not an AVA guy. I follow the grapes from vineyard to vineyard," says David, who has more than 20 vintages behind him. The head winemaker's eclectic approach has earned Bridlewood Estate Winery a highly revered standing for Central Coast wines.

In addition to the suite of chardonnay and pinot noir, the Bridlewood portfolio includes award-winning syrah, including the small-production estate syrah, which highlights the exceptional fruit of Bridlewood's home vineyard. David has also introduced a reserve chardonnay and pinot noir from the Santa Lucia Highlands. Tasting room guests and Winner's Circle wine club members can experience the full spectrum of Bridlewood's collection, including exclusive, limited-production syrah, pinot noir and red wine blends.

Top Left: Set on a high bench of ancient seabed where limestone pebbles pepper the vineyards, estate vines enjoy cool nights and long, sunny days.
Photograph courtesy of Bridlewood Estate Winery

Middle Left: Oak is used as a backdrop to the flavors of the wine; barrel room casks are from France, Eastern Europe and the United States.
Photograph courtesy of Bridlewood Estate Winery

Bottom Left: The state-of-the-art winery has pneumatic bladder presses, temperature-controlled fermenters and gentle grape and wine handling systems for producing exceptional wines.
Photograph by Peter Malinowski

Facing Page: The Bridlewood Estate Winery portfolio offers an array of exceptional wines from the approachable Central Coast tier to exclusive tasting room-only wines.
Photograph by Joel Ottersbach

Bridlewood takes full advantage of the region's diverse terroir and ideal grape-growing conditions, always looking ahead to new varietals and blends that showcase the land's diversity, while elevating the Central Coast onto the world stage.

WINE & FARE

Bridlewood Monterey County Chardonnay

Pair with raw oysters, scallops, white pasta sauces and polenta.

Bridlewood Central Coast Syrah

Pair with grilled red meats, leg of lamb and wild game such as venison.

Bridlewood Reserve Viognier

Pair with lobster, crab, abalone, pâté, fresh fruit and a variety of hard and soft cheeses.

Bridlewood Estate Syrah

Pair with pheasant, steak, grilled mushrooms and sheep's milk cheeses.

Tastings

Open to the public daily, year-round

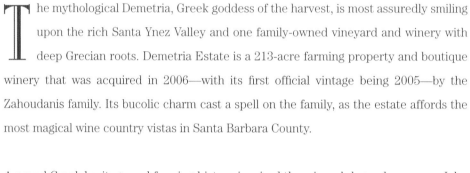

Demetria Estate

Los Olivos

The mythological Demetria, Greek goddess of the harvest, is most assuredly smiling upon the rich Santa Ynez Valley and one family-owned vineyard and winery with deep Grecian roots. Demetria Estate is a 213-acre farming property and boutique winery that was acquired in 2006—with its first official vintage being 2005—by the Zahoudanis family. Its bucolic charm cast a spell on the family, as the estate affords the most magical wine country vistas in Santa Barbara County.

A proud Greek heritage and farming history inspired the winery's legendary name; John Zahoudanis' grandfather grew and harvested plentiful wheat crops, olives and winegrapes in his native Greece a century ago. John arrived in America when the Zahoudanis family immigrated with dreams of a different life post-World War II, eventually settling in southern California. After a long career as a developer, John's own vision of becoming a vintner and running a winery came to fruition. Today the family lives on the estate sharing a passion for the winemaking lifestyle.

Los Olivos is in the heart of the Santa Ynez Valley AVA, known for its fertile soils and long, cool growing season, a blessing to Demetria's 45 acres of vineyard blocks. The Santa Rita Hills is an east-west mountain chain that has characteristic early morning fog, sunny days and chilly nights with coastal winds coming inland off the Pacific Ocean. As a

Left: Demetria Estate's vineyards and the family winery are nestled above Foxen Canyon.
Photographs by Justin Crane Vandenberg

Facing Page: Young syrah vines flourish in the Santa Ynez Valley.
Photograph by Peter Malinowski

result, the estate vineyard yields abundant harvests in October, much later than other California regions, producing red varietals including syrah, grenache and mourvèdre and white varietals such as viognier, marsanne, roussanne and grenache blanc. Demetria Estate has earned a reputation for Rhône-style wines, all handcrafted by winemaker Michael Roth. Michael's Old World, traditional methods of artisanal winemaking have been well received from coast to coast, enjoyed in both homes and restaurants. Also a culinary enthusiast, it was Michael's love of food that directed him toward wine. Michael's winemaking style focuses on producing earthy and structured wines with low alcohol and high acidity that perfectly complement a variety of gourmet fare.

Michael is a purist and an environmentalist who firmly believes in organically grown and biodynamically farmed vineyards, avoiding pesticides, using native yeasts for fermentation and maintaining minimal intervention. Michael ages delectable vintages in French oak barrels to allow only the true taste of the terroir to come through. A cult

Above Left: Demetria's tasting room and patio overlook the grounds.

Above Right: The eastward view reveals a panorama of rolling hills.

Facing Page: Burgundy and Rhône-style wines, among Demetria's other offerings, are best enjoyed on the patio.
Photographs by Peter Malinowski

following has formed and Demetria Estate's Wine Society members look forward to receiving low-production, limited release "society only" wines while visitors can book private tastings to sample the Old World charm and artistic excellence expressed in every bottle.

DEMETRIA

WINE & FARE

Demetria 2006 Chardonnay

Pair with hazelnut chicken in a prosciutto-parmesan cream sauce.

Demetria 2006 Cuvee Sandra Pinot Noir

Pair with duck breast, roasted peaches and walnut-parsley risotto.

Demetria 2006 North Slope Syrah

Pair with caramelized shallot and thyme-crusted rack of lamb.

Demetria 2007 Bon Bon
(50% viognier, 50% roussanne)

Pair with roasted fig and honey tart with lavender-infused whipped cream.

Tastings
Open by appointment only

Kenneth Volk Vineyards

Santa Maria Valley

Firmly rooted as a third-generation Californian, Kenneth Volk developed a passion for horticulture and gardening while tending the orchard at his family's home. His true love for nurturing and growing became manifest during more than 30 years as an expert viticulturist working some of the most diverse terroirs of the vast Central Coast, from northern AVAs of the Lime Kiln Valley, Monterey and Paso Robles, to the southern appellations of Santa Maria Valley and Santa Ynez Valley. The president and director of winemaking at his namesake winery—Kenneth Volk Vineyards, Ken takes the practice of grape-growing to an unprecedented level.

Perhaps best known as the founder of the legendary Wild Horse Winery and Vineyards in Templeton, California, Ken helped build the reputation of the Central Coast growing region with this renowned brand for over two decades. After selling the Wild Horse Winery and Vineyards in 2003 he acquired the original Byron Winery in 2004—formerly owned by Robert Mondavi—located in the cool Santa Maria Valley AVA of Santa Barbara County. Ken has enjoyed returning to small-scale winemaking and taking his craft to a higher level of quality, producing an array of varieties, including a selection of vineyard designated chardonnay and pinot noir, at his new winery. Ken also enjoys working with many different grape varieties, including varieties he deems "heirloom," such as malvasia bianca, verdelho, negrette and other difficult-to-pronounce varieties. He is a fruit scientist, a creative winemaker and an artist of sorts, with the most comprehensive wine portfolio in the region.

Top Left: The beauty of nature abounds on the grounds of the vineyards.
Photograph by Maria Villano

Middle Left: Innovative winemaker Kenneth Volk personally oversees the planting, growing and harvesting of his prized varietals.
Photograph courtesy of Kenneth Volk Vineyards

Bottom Left: Bottles bear the Kenneth Volk golden monogram seal of quality.
Photograph by Maria Villano

Facing Page: Kenneth Volk artisan wines are matured in natural oak barrels for up to 18 months in order to reach the peak of perfection.
Photograph courtesy of Kenneth Volk Vineyards

Ken is especially proud of the vineyard he manages in the Lime Kiln Valley AVA. The Enz Vineyard was originally planted in 1895. The old vine mourvèdre and zinfandel are head-trained, dry-farmed and produce delicious and distinctive wines.

Ken's passionate understanding of the natural history and climate of the Central Coast has given him a unique perspective to selecting superior vineyards for each variety he produces. Kenneth Volk Vineyards' location in the Santa Maria Valley is surrounded by some of the finest vineyards for chardonnay and pinot noir in California. Surrounding vineyards include Bien Nacido, Julia's, Sierra Madre, William Garey, Solomon Hills, Riverbench and Nielson. The Santa Maria Valley is unique in that the valley runs in an east to west direction, making it one of the coolest wine regions in California. Cold marine air flows in from San Luis Bay across the Guadalupe dunes into the Santa Maria

Valley maintaining a cool climate grape-growing area. The cool growing conditions in the Santa Maria Valley allow for one of the longest grape-growing seasons in California and gradual maturation of traditional Burgundy varieties.

A combination of outstanding vineyards and innovative winemaking techniques is the secret behind Kenneth Volk Vineyards' uniquely styled wines. Kenneth Volk Vineyards offers myriad selections through

Above: Scenic vistas, flower-lined walkways and an inviting tasting room create unforgettable experiences for guests.
Above left photograph courtesy of Kenneth Volk Vineyards
Above right photograph by Maria Villano

Facing Page: The KVV Cellar Door Club offers a vast portfolio of wines ideal to share and pair with favorite gourmet dishes.
Photograph courtesy of Kenneth Volk Vineyards

its Cellar Door Club, a first-of-its-kind concept where members can customize their quarterly shipments from one of the finest collections of wines in California.

Ken is a veritable founding father of the Central Coast's wine industry and has served the community as president and chairman of the board for the Paso Robles Vintners and Growers Association and was the founding president of the Paso Robles Grape Growers Association. He and his wife Tricia reside in San Luis Obispo with their children, Kenny and Valentina.

WINE & FARE

Bien Nacido Vineyard Pinot Noir
(100% pinot noir)
Pair with cedar plank seared wild salmon.

San Bernabe Vineyard Malvasia Bianca
Pair with ginger-and-mustard-glazed albacore tuna.

Jaybird Chardonnay
Pair with a vegetarian risotto Milanese entrée.

Enz Vineyard Mourvèdre
Pair with confit de canard.

Tastings
Open to the public daily, year-round

Zaca Mesa Winery & Vineyards

Los Olivos

The word zaca in the Native American Chumash language means peaceful place. Part of a historical 1830s Spanish Land Grant, the original Rancho La Zaca piece of earth is now the property on which Zaca Mesa Winery & Vineyards stands, a serene place with a sense of history and lore that inspires. Its regional flavor is something that transcends time and is captured in every bottle of wine produced from vines grown on complex soils.

Thirty miles from the Pacific in Santa Barbara County, Zaca Mesa Winery & Vineyards is situated in the northern Santa Ynez Valley AVA. The terroir possesses qualities that support premium grape-growing. Known for its sandy loam with limestone elements, the original vineyard was planted in 1973 with treasured Rhône varietals. Mother Nature is responsible for nurturing today's vines on 200 acres of the 750-acre winery site, thriving with syrah, grenache, grenache blanc, mourvèdre, viognier, cinsault, roussanne and chardonnay. Tight spacing forces the vines to work harder and struggle a bit, producing concentrated fruit bursting with delicious character. "Our award-winning wines are balanced and have a unique richness because of where we grow our fruit," says Zaca Mesa president Brook Williams. He uses the analogy that tomatoes in one backyard taste different than those grown in someone else's backyard. Quite a simple farmer's observation, but the ideal terroir is the veritable secret to Zaca Mesa's gold-medal releases, all masterfully handcrafted by head winemaker Eric Mohseni since 2007.

Top Left: Zaca Mesa's labels identify the exclusively estate-grown and estate-bottled wines.
Photograph by Peter Malinowski

Middle Left: Winemaker Eric Mohseni and vineyard foreman Ruben Camacho take a break from picking grenache blanc at harvest time.
Photograph courtesy of Zaca Mesa Winery

Bottom Left: Zaca Mesa wines are matured in seasoned French oak barrels to impart subtle flavors.
Photograph by Peter Malinowski

Facing Page: A southeast view of high-elevation Mesa B block thrives with syrah vines planted in 2004.
Photograph by Peter Malinowski

Syrah is one of the vineyard's longstanding varietals, as Zaca Mesa was the first to plant syrah vines in Santa Barbara County early on in 1978. The winery has received high honors for its 1993 syrah—being the only Central Coast vintage ever included on the coveted *Wine Spectator*'s annual Top 10 list of exciting wines—earning outstanding 90-plus ratings and enthusiastic reviews from the editors. On another notable occasion, the award-winning Zaca Mesa Syrah was served at a special 1996 White House dinner for President Clinton and French President Chirac. Proud of its 30-year syrah-growing heritage, Zaca Mesa now cultivates over 90 acres of prized estate syrah, harvested to make new releases for novice drinkers to seasoned connoisseurs.

At an elevation of 1,500 feet, Zaca Mesa is nestled amid a transverse mountain range extending to the ocean that provides the maritime climate; vines welcome being above the fog-line with more sunshine and cooler temperatures than other growing regions. The vineyards are actually planted on top of two mesas. Zaca Mesa's vineyards are entirely farmed using sustainable practices to be kind to the environment, and fruit enjoys consistent ripening thanks to the weather. Traditional winemakers with an Old World approach, the vintners grow fruit in the purest way to create wines requiring minimal manipulation. Estate-grown and estate-bottled Zaca Mesa wines are 100-percent derived from this property and never leave until after bottling. The eco-conscious winery produces 25,000 to 35,000 cases annually, distributed in 45 states and internationally.

Above Left: The winery gate is marked by an old farm windmill, a tribute to the vineyard's rich agricultural roots.
Photograph by Peter Malinowski

Above Right: Looking southward, the Cushman block of viognier appears to go on forever.
Photograph by Andy Katz

Facing Page: Zaca Mesa's award-winning syrah and viognier are perfectly paired with gourmet delights.
Photograph by Deborah Denker

Zaca Mesa was first established by the Cushman family who set the precedent for being good stewards of the land, and today the vineyards and boutique winery have become a Central Coast tour destination. A quaint nine-mile drive down a bumpy road from Los Olivos brings visitors in to experience Zaca Mesa. The welcoming tasting room is housed in a rustic barn where guests enjoy new releases and delight in the sights and sounds of the mesa with its native sagebrush, mature oaks, and abundant wildlife; an enchanting place that emanates a true sense of what California's Central Coast is all about.

WINE & FARE

Zaca Mesa Viognier
Pair with grilled trout and Asian or spicy cuisine.

Zaca Mesa Roussanne
Pair with grilled halibut or herb roasted chicken.

Zaca Mesa Z Cuvée
(blend of grenache, mourvèdre and syrah)
Pair with a variety of foods, from mushroom pizza to rosemary crusted rack of lamb.

Zaca Mesa Syrah
Pair with grilled and roasted meats or bold imported cheeses.

Tastings
Open to the public daily, year-round

Jason-Stephens Winery, page 178

Léal Vineyards, page 180

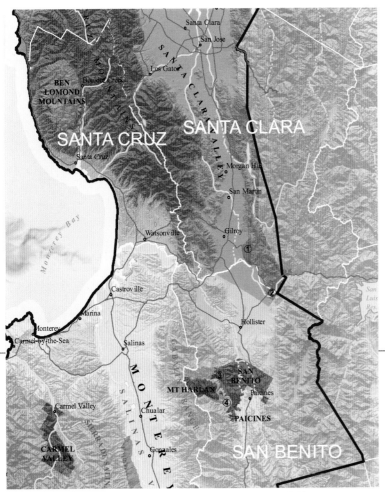

San Benito and Santa Clara

Counties

Calera Wine Company

Hollister

J osh Jensen, founder and winemaker of Calera Wine Company, was tenacious. Skeptics said that growing prized, complex pinot noir grapes and wines could not be done in America, but Calera has proved to unbelievers that the opposite was true.

Josh was fortunate to have been introduced to the great Burgundies and Bordeaux at a very young age by Dr. George Selleck, a lifelong family friend and respected wine expert in San Francisco. A native Californian, Josh went east for college, to Yale, where he earned his degree in world history, and then on to Oxford, receiving a master's in anthropology. But when it came time to choose a career, he was not drawn to the usual fields of medicine, law, banking and the like. Instead, to many people's surprise, he wanted to grow grapes and make wine. To begin the learning process, Josh worked for 10 days as a humble grape picker in Burgundy at Domaine de la Romanée-Conti in 1970, and also had a short apprenticeship the following year at Domaine Dujac in Morey-St.-Denis. Inspired by his Côte d'Or experience, Josh returned home to California and started looking for land rich with limestone deposits; Burgundian masters shared that limestone soil was the secret to growing the best, most complex pinot noir and chardonnay grapes.

From the first brush and tree clearing, planting and initial winemaking in 1975, Josh set his vineyards and winery, named Calera, on an extremely traditional, Old World course using the classic methods he observed at top domaines in Burgundy. His methods employed whole cluster fermentation utilizing only native yeast species, little or no racking and handling of wines during barrel maturation, complete malolactic fermentation for all

Top Left: Calera's founder-owner Josh Jensen has been a pioneer in the region and was instrumental in forming the Mount Harlan AVA.

Middle Left: Old World-style wines patiently develop in row-upon-row of imported French oak barrels.

Bottom Left: Calera's limekiln logo is branded onto every oak barrel, a reminder of the land's rich history.

Facing Page: Guests are awestruck at the spectacular vista looking southeast from the winery's picnic area.
Photographs by Maria Villano

wines, and zero filtration for the pinot noirs. Josh's winemaking goal and philosophy has always been to make true, honest expressions of the grape. The very design of Calera's unique hillside winery building, constructed on seven different levels, utilizing four original concrete retaining walls from an abandoned 1950s era limestone crushing plant, symbolizes its commitment to moving the wines from one stage to the next by the gentlest possible means: the natural flow of gravity.

Today Calera is recognized for its unique high elevation vineyards on the slopes of Mt. Harlan. The winery petitioned the U.S. government to create the Mt. Harlan American Viticultural Area, which was officially approved in 1990. Calera still owns the only vineyards in this extremely rugged, remote 7,400-acre appellation in the western-most part of San Benito County, about 25 miles inland from the Pacific Ocean.

This trailblazing winery has garnered a strong international reputation by producing pure, complex, balanced and intense pinot noirs, chardonnays and viogniers for more than three decades. In 1973, Josh petitioned the United States government to import viognier cuttings, as the variety was not yet grown on American soil. The U.S. government worked in collaboration with UC Davis to import the revered vines from the tiny northern Rhône Valley town of Condrieu; it took 15 years before the first plants were

Top Left: The fog-shrouded view of Jensen Vineyard features 100% pinot noir originally planted in 1975.

Middle Left: Josh's natural process uses fermentation tanks and presses on a seven-level, hillside gravity-flow winery.

Bottom Left: Rustic bottle racks in Calera's tasting room offer visitors a world-class selection.

Facing Page: Pure expressions of the grape, Calera handcrafted wines have received accolades at home and abroad.
Photographs by Maria Villano

offered to California growers in 1988. For 20 years and counting, Calera's viognier is touted as a remarkable, aromatic white wine meant to be enjoyed young. By contrast, Calera's pinots and chardonnays can be bottle-aged for many years, allowing further complexities to develop for pleasing the most discerning palate.

Josh's artful craft has been industry-recognized: He was named Winemaker of the Year in 2007 by *The San Francisco Chronicle*, and the following year Calera was celebrated as Winery of the Year by *Wine & Spirits* magazine. Today Calera's winemaking mission remains the same as it was in 1975: "We work to make the absolute best damn tasting wines we can from our special plots of ground."

WINE & FARE

Calera Mt. Harlan Chardonnay
(100% chardonnay)

Pair with grilled salmon, roasted rosemary chicken or pasta with shellfish.

Calera Mt. Harlan Viognier
(100% viognier)

Pair with sushi and sashimi, foie gras, spicy shellfish or lobster with drawn butter.

Calera Central Coast Pinot Noir
(100% pinot noir)

Pair with soups, beef, pork or more casual fare.

Calera Ryan Vineyard, Mt. Harlan Pinot Noir
(100% pinot noir)

Pair with fowl dishes such as duck confit, herb-roasted pheasant and squab.

Tastings
Open to the public daily, year-round

Guglielmo Winery

Morgan Hill

A winemaking pioneer in the agriculturally rich Santa Clara Valley near Morgan Hill, Emilio Guglielmo planted a dream that began in 1925 when he founded his namesake winery. Born in 1883 near Asti in Italy's Piedmonte region, Emilio invested in his future by purchasing vineyard land just 80 miles south of San Francisco. Today the winery is family-owned and operated by a third generation of Guglielmos; Emilio's grandsons George E., Gene and Gary oversee the vineyards and winery, continuing a passionate winemaking tradition.

Italian-style wines were Emilio's first creations and his robust red wines began to have an enthusiastic following. In the late 1940s the winery was passed on to Emilio's son, George W. Guglielmo and his wife Madeline. Working together, the couple expanded the winery's estate vineyards as well as distribution, while retaining the family's commitment to quality, distinctive tastes and value. This winery has evolved with the production of award-winning, premium varietal wines derived from annual harvests grown on 100 acres of loamy soils on the family's estate vineyards: 70-year-old zinfandel along with 30- to 50-year-old petite sirah and grignolino grapevines. "The fruit speaks for itself," says resident winemaker George Guglielmo. "Our diverse wines truly express the traditions of my family's cultural heritage." The Guglielmo experience begins as you step onto the cobblestone piazza and hear the village fountain, reminiscent of the family's Piedmontese homeland. Visitors feel at home as they take in the charming tasting room and gift shop, Villa Emile Event Center and picturesque grounds—truly a special place to celebrate "one of life's simple pleasures" with a toast to family values.

Top Left: The original sign depicts the partnership of founder Emilio with son George W., continuing the family's winery heritage.
Photograph by Zabrina Tipton

Middle Left: Dedicated to winery founder Emilio Guglielmo, Villa Emile Event Center hosts weddings and corporate events.
Photograph by Custom Creations Photography

Bottom Left: The winery's Piazza d' Madellena and its village fountain pay homage to Madeline, matriarch of the Guglielmo family.
Photograph by Custom Creations Photography

Facing Page: The hills of Santa Clara Valley provide a beautiful backdrop for early morning views of old zinfandel vines.
Photograph by Zabrina Tipton

Jason–Stephens Winery

Gilroy

Nestled in the Santa Clara Valley appellation, just 13 miles from the Pacific, lies a river bed canyon only half a mile wide. Small but sweet, the fruitful Uvas Valley terroir mirrors France's Rhône Valley where world-class wines are born. Jason-Stephens Winery was founded by winemaker Jason Goelz and estate vineyard grower Stephen Dorcich, solidifying the partnership between a visionary entrepreneur and an experienced California viticulturist. The winery's Uvas Ranch vineyard was previously a peach orchard but destiny prevailed; the Spanish word uvas means "grapes" and the agricultural region bears the ideal climate characterized by cooling marine fogs, with warm, dry summers, creating the perfect balance for grape-growing success.

Jason is one of the youngest winemakers on the Central Coast. As a teenager he was inspired after touring Napa with his mother, catching his first glimpse into the winemaking world; he soon attended Cal Poly for wine and viticulture studies. Today he focuses his energy on winemaking with intense passion. The Jason-Stephens state-of-the-art winery has an air of sophistication with a decidedly hip edge reflecting its current heritage. Yet, in each bottle, Jason and Steve have captured the fine art of winemaking blended with the science of transforming raw grapes into pleasing wines. The duo's mission is to create a diverse selection of wines that stimulate the mind, soul and especially the palate, through their form of alchemy. Today the award-winning estate winery crafts more than 9,000 cases annually of distinct Santa Clara Valley varietals: cabernet sauvignon, syrah, merlot, zinfandel, chardonnay, cabernet franc, malbec, petit verdot and mourvèdre—engaging wines that can be enjoyed everyday among family and friends.

Top Left: Labels have lettering to represent an intertwining of winemaker and winegrower, the owners' complementary talents.

Middle Left: Vintners Stephen and Jason oversee rows of bountiful grapevines on the palm-lined drive of Uvas Ranch vineyards.

Bottom Left: Oak barrels once used for maturation are stacked on the winery's vintage truck; the size, age and toasting of the casks are key factors that impart subtle flavors into the wine.

Facing Page: A year-round outdoor patio overlooks scenic vistas; spring bud break is especially picture-perfect for sipping new vintages and lingering for hours.
Photographs by Maria Villano

Léal Vineyards

Hollister

Léal Vineyards is certainly not your average winery. Where else can you go and sample fine wines in an environment surrounded by relaxed California sophistication and mingle with hip wine lovers? Léal Vineyards is the enthusiastic creation of owner-winemaker Frank Léal. His nonchalant winemaking mantra goes like this: Phat wines—no pretense. The entrepreneurial vintner is a nonconformist in California wine country, and wine lovers like his unorthodox thinking.

Frank's mission is to fashion truly exceptional wines that appeal to the connoisseur and novice alike. He went from being your basic blue-collar guy to realizing his dream when he acquired the scenic 45-acre Léal estate. On this coveted vineyard, with its amazing soils and unique microclimate, Frank passionately grows San Benito County AVA chardonnay, merlot, cabernet sauvignon, malbec, syrah, grenache and mourvèdre. Nestled in the rolling foothills of Hollister in California's Central Coast region, the premier winery was hand built in 1999 with an eye to both tradition and cutting-edge winemaking methods.

Léal Vineyards is known for producing limited, award-winning wines meant for good times. Considered the "in-spot" for tastings, events and weddings, Léal has an unconventional personality, thanks to Frank's forward attitude. The winery's vibe is definitely rock star, and passionate wine lovers have helped to put Léal's artisan wines at the top of the charts.

Top Left: Léal wine bottle corks are all natural and imported from Portugal.

Bottom Left: The Léal estate cabernet sauvignon block is a bit of heaven in Hollister.

Facing Page: Stone steps descend from the winery to a picturesque pond replete with white swans.
Photographs by Maria Villano

Frank is committed to crafting vintages that rival European fine wines in their expression of the region and chic quafability. Celebrities like Emeril Lagasse and Kid Rock have also partied at Léal Vineyards, tasted the edgy vintner's creations and grown fond of the trend-setting wine label.

Frank approaches winemaking as a freestyle art form rather than a scientific task. He is big on experimentation to ensure that the very best wine is produced from each vintage of precious estate grapes, which are harvested based on flavor rather than numbers. During each vintage, multiple sources of oak barrels are tested prior to selection, imported from France, Hungary, Russia, China and sourced within America. Multiple fermenting yeast strains are also tested with each grape varietal. The goal is to make the best possible wine by not following a recipe. It is Frank's highly creative, perfectionist approach that sets his wines apart.

Many of Léal's wines are bottled unfiltered. Although it is a controversial method with considerable risks, Frank believes that his approach is the best way to display their full, complex potential. The wines of Léal are phat and robust with deep extraction, delivering huge flavor, silky texture and a long, full finish. And while they consistently win more than their share of accolades and awards, they are specifically designed

Top Left: Guests are impressed by Lavánda, a state-of-the-art events venue, surrounded by sweet blooming lavender.

Middle Left: The tasting room is the perfect spot to sample new Léal vintages and engage in lively conversation.

Bottom Left: Oak casks are filled with aging wine in Léal Vineyards' estate barrel room.

Facing Page: Frank Léal's award-winning artisan wines excite the palate with their phat, robust flavors.
Photographs by María Villano

to please Léal's loyal fans. Work hard, play hard may seem cliché but at Léal Vineyards the philosophy lives and is expressed in each fantastic drop. Frank invites all to "Pull a cork, shake your booty and celebrate fine wines and good times."

WINE & FARE

Léal Vineyards Estate Chardonnay
(70% barrel-fermented, 30% stainless-steel fermented)
Pair with pan-seared scallops with ginger-orange spinach.

Léal Vineyards Threesome
(70% syrah, 20% grenache, 10% mourvèdre)
Pair with herb-marinated rack of lamb.

Léal Vineyards Godsend
(100% estate cabernet sauvignon)
Pair with grilled, aged prime ribeye steak.

Tastings
Open to the public daily, year-round

Sarah's Vineyard

Gilroy

Imagine an eccentric scientist turned serious premium winemaker. Tim Slater, a Silicon Valley success story and prolific inventor, made a radical 180-degree turnaround to pursue his newfound dream after the dot-com bust in the '90s and to escape the frenetic technology industry. Tim has always been a connoisseur of fine food, French wine and great music; the romance of owning a winery captured his attention when he learned that an established Santa Clara Valley AVA estate vineyard was on the market. Central Coast pioneer Marilyn Sarah Clark had built a national reputation with her namesake Sarah's Vineyard since 1978 but decided to pass the baton after 20 productive years. Tim seized the kismet opportunity by acquiring the 28-acre vineyard.

Tim's inspirational philosophy has become a poetic mantra: "Wine is the music from the vineyard." He appreciates the complex soils and marine-influenced microclimate that the southwest corner of Santa Clara Valley affords his vines. Tucked on a gentle slope at the eastern foot of Mount Madonna near a windy mountain pass, the terroir has a rich history of producing prized pinot noir and chardonnay varietals that flourish thanks to foggy mornings and hot sunny afternoons, moderated by strong ocean breezes and cool nights. Tim was enamored by the year-round green lushness and exceptionally fertile beauty of the region in the foothills just a few miles from the dusty little town of Gilroy. Years ago, before Silicon Valley development ate up the land, the Santa Clara Valley was a thriving farming area known for cherries, apricots, plums and almonds. Sarah's Vineyard is one of the remaining farms in the region, and perhaps Santa Clara Valley's best-kept secret. Tim produces estate-grown winegrapes on 17 acres of his vineyards; Burgundian and Rhône

Top Left: Tucked in the rural southwestern corner of Silicon Valley, Sarah's Vineyard has produced premium Burgundian and Rhône-style wines for over three decades.

Middle Left: Founded in 1978, Sarah's Vineyard celebrated its 30th harvest in 2007.

Bottom Left: Proprietor Tim Slater, a former Silicon Valley researcher, is a familiar face in the tasting room.

Facing Page: As seen from an estate walking trail, springtime blossoms in the pinot noir vineyard against a backdrop of nearby hills.
Photographs by Maria Villano

varietals are also sourced from local vineyards in the Santa Cruz Mountains appellation a few miles west of the estate. Just a few hundred yards east, the pre-Prohibition, Besson family vineyard provides old vine grenache and zinfandel, which are used for varietals and blends. Other varietals Tim grows alongside his mainstay pinot noir and chardonnay include syrah, grenache, roussanne, viognier and marsanne, to name a few.

Elegant Burgundian-style wines inspired by his affinity for traditional French winemaking methods are Tim's forte. Sarah's Vineyard syrah has earned a coveted 90 point ranking from Robert Parker. *The San Francisco Chronicle* Wine Competition awarded a gold to the 2007 estate pinot noir, with double-gold and best of class medals for the 2007 Santa Cruz Mountains pinot noir and 2005 syrah. Winemaker Ken Deis, with decades of experience making ultra premium pinot noir, now masterfully creates Rhône-inspired blends of grenache, carignane and syrah—emulating much admired Châteauneuf-du-Pape blends—named Côte de Madone to pay tribute to its impressive geographic heritage. Tim is also a chef at heart who studied the art of Provençal cooking at Le Cordon Bleu Paris. He loves to serve new vintages with gastronomic delights at home and recommends his food-friendly wines with proper gourmet pairings so they sing in perfect harmony.

Top Left: Relaxed and rustic, the quaint tasting room and art gallery is housed in a 50-year-old former horse barn.

Middle Left: Early bud break in the fertile vineyards symbolizes a healthy harvest ahead.

Bottom Left: A view above the estate vineyard to the mountains beyond shows the serene beauty of this hidden corner of Silicon Valley.

Facing Page: Award-winning Rhône-inspired blends and varietals pair with gourmet fare to please the most discerning palates.
Photographs by Maria Villano

Visitors to Sarah's Vineyard can experience the magic of grape growing and sip wine in a rustic barn tasting room reminiscent of the area's rural roots. The charming boutique winery is staffed by genuinely hospitable people in a relaxed atmosphere replete with a redwood deck, wood-fired pizza oven, picnic grounds and competition bocce ball courts. Friday nights are festive at Sarah's Vineyard, where locals and coastal travelers meet for conviviality and a glass of award-winning pinot.

WINE & FARE

Sarah's Vineyard 2008 Côte de Madone Blanc
(marsanne, roussanne, viognier and grenache blanc)

Pair with poached scallops in court bouillon, served on a bed of sautéed leek julienne.

Sarah's Vineyard 2007 Estate Pinot Noir
(100% pinot noir)

Pair with a simple bistro steak smothered in mushrooms and caramelized onions.

Sarah's Vineyard 2005 Syrah
(100% estate syrah)

Pair with roasted leg of lamb rubbed with olive oil, garlic, thyme and rosemary.

Sarah's Vineyard Estate Chardonnay
(100% estate chardonnay)

Prepare a light dessert of ripe comice Pear-Chardonnay sorbet, sweetened with honey.

Tastings
Open to the public daily, year-round

From being entrepreneurs in the cut-flower world to creating vats of homemade wine as a hobby, the Vanni family has evolved much like their wines. While living in the heart of Santa Clara Valley, the birthplace of Northern California's wine country, Dave and Valerie Vanni had a dream to one day establish a winery, purchasing what was originally the renowned Bertero property owned by veteran viticulturists since the 1920s. In 1989 the Vannis began creating award-winning wines expressed from fruitful yields grown on their historic Rancho de Solis. Appropriately named, Solis Winery bears the Spanish word derived from Latin, which means sun. Fall harvests come from a sun-drenched 16-acre vineyard and another 25-acre family vineyard. Solis Winery grape varietals include cabernet sauvignon, cabernet franc, merlot, chardonnay, syrah, sangiovese, fiano, muscat canelli and zinfandel.

Today brothers Vic and Michael Vanni run the roll-up-your-sleeves, small-production vineyard in this prime agricultural region—with the Santa Cruz mountain range as its backdrop—where grapes reap the benefit of sunny days, cool nights and morning fog. The appellation is known for a rare microclimate with lots of sun and coastal effect breezes; ideal conditions for growing superior winegrapes. Winemaker Michael has earned a reputation for handcrafting gold medal varietals and blends such as Tuscan-inspired sangiovese and classic Bordeaux-style merlot vintages. But it is southern Italy's classical Avellino fiano white that has brought Solis Winery into the limelight alongside its flagship Meritage blend Cara Mia. The Vannis' artisan wines express Italian and French traditions using respected Old World practices. The creative family works from "soil to bottle," serving 4,000 cases of wine annually in an atmosphere of warmth and pride.

Top Left: An Old World barrel end is a charming memento of the area's long-standing winemaking history.

Middle Left: Located on scenic Hecker Pass Highway, the Solis sign attracts many California travelers.

Bottom Left: Each capsule foil features the artfully embossed Solis script logo.

Facing Page: Estate sangiovese vines in early spring enjoy a lush mountain backdrop and perfect climate.
Photographs by Maria Villano

Sycamore Creek
Vineyards & Winery

Morgan Hill

One of the Central Coast's best-kept secrets is Sycamore Creek Vineyards & Winery. On the southern fringes of Santa Clara Valley AVA in the heart of the Uvas Valley sits a small, family-owned vineyard tucked amid the Santa Cruz Mountains. In 2005, Bill and Carolyn Holt acquired the creekside property—originally the Marchetti Ranch and winery that closed during Prohibition and was reopened in 1975 as Sycamore Creek. From day one the Holts' son-in-law Ted Mederios became the master winemaker and manager of the estate vineyards. With a passion for growing premium winegrapes and crafting distinctive wines, Ted and Bill control quality so the utmost can be expressed from the intense fruit, transforming clusters into gold medal-winning wines. Main varietals include old vine plantings of cabernet sauvignon and chardonnay. They employ state-of-the-art trellising and canopy management techniques on Uvas Valley Vineyard, which is planted with cabernet sauvignon, petit verdot, malbec and cabernet franc.

Just seven miles from Monterey Bay, the vineyards bask in a coveted place ideal for growing Bordeaux-style varietals. The microclimate is overcast in the morning, clear and warm in the afternoon and cool at night, providing optimal conditions for producing premium winegrapes. Ted philosophizes, "Winemaking is really done out in the vineyard by growing the best fruit; the cellar part is simple." He makes it all sound easy, but his strict attention to the vines is a family affair. Ted and his wife Tammie have trellised, pruned and irrigated some of the vineyards themselves. The first planting was a two-acre block they named Dragonfly, located next to Uvas Creek on Uvas Valley Vineyard soils. Capturing the romance of the abundant region, Sycamore Creek's handcrafted wines are celebrated through weekend educational camps, friendly harvest parties and lively grape stomps.

Top Left: Popped corks: evidence of a festive evening at the Sycamore Creek tasting room.

Middle Left: Modern canopy management and vineyard practices assure superior-quality Bordeaux varietal harvests from Uvas Valley Vineyard.

Bottom Left: Sycamore Creek's family includes winemaker-general manager Ted Medeiros, proprietors Bill and Carolyn Holt with Suzie Holt and Tammie Medeiros. Syrah, the winery dog, greets guests.

Facing Page: The charming winery, cellar and tasting room sit quietly on Sycamore Creek amid the dry-farmed, old vine cabernet sauvignon.
Photographs by Maria Villano

Thomas Fogarty Winery & Vineyard, page 200

Soquel Vineyards, page 198

Santa Cruz and San Mateo Counties

David Bruce Winery

Los Gatos

David Bruce Winery has earned an international reputation for its dedication to producing some of the greatest pinot noir and chardonnay in the world. David and Jeannette's working philosophy reflects the winery's status, and everyone involved in the family-owned winemaking enterprise shares their passion expressed in the mantra "taste our dedication." Thanks to a committed team of professionals, the winery has received accolades for vintages of superior quality and quaffability, with exceptional color, an incomparable velvety texture and fruit-forwardness.

The vision did it all! David explains: "In my formative years as a dermatologist, I had a life-changing experience. I was reading about Burgundy and Romanée-Conti, the most famous vineyard in the world. In *Wines of France*, Alexis Lichine described these wines as having a noble robe. I was so struck by this strange phrase that I had to find out, firsthand, what it meant." On opening that bottle the whole room was pervaded by a floral, spicy aroma. David's vision, as he drank that wine, was of a vineyard on top of a mountain. "I was making the greatest pinot noir in the whole world! This inspired who we are, why we are and what we are." David Bruce Winery produces a gift for mankind. It is the Bruces' heartfelt task here on earth—they call it a rite of passage. In 50 years one can do a lot. "Wines really are made naturally in the vineyard, but you must be very careful when crafting it in the winery," emphasizes David.

David founded his namesake winery in the early 1960s; he chose the remote Santa Cruz Mountains and was one of the first of a new generation that would lead a resurgence of premium winemaking in this region. After completing his medical residency, David purchased 40 acres of land above the fog-line in the Santa Cruz Mountains. He cleared

Top Left: Jeannette and David Bruce are involved in all aspects of the winery operations.

Bottom Left & Facing Page: From vineyard to bottle, the Los Gatos winery adheres to traditional European practices. *Photographs by M.J. Wickham*

the land himself and planted the vineyard by hand. Since then, David Bruce Winery has become well-known for its single-pointed dedication to producing the greatest pinot noir in the world. In pursuit of this goal, the winery has adhered to traditional European practices under the direction of David and Jeannette and the staff that trace back to the ancestral pioneers of winemaking in the Santa Cruz Mountains and Santa Clara Valley.

The winery's artisanal wines are produced from varietals grown on the 2,200-foot elevation, 25-acre Santa Cruz Mountains estate vineyard or fruit sourced from the best growers in Northern and Central California. Having a breadth and diversity of grape sources has allowed David Bruce Winery to create a broad range of wines and firmly establishes the vintner as one of the leading premium winemakers on the international stage.

David Bruce Winery has also been in the forefront of efforts to develop innovative new methods that have changed the face of winemaking in California. David is recognized as a leader in the use of whole-berry fermentation, one of the first winemakers to import French oak barrels and an early advocate of foot crushing and small-barrel fermentation. His blend of passion with scientific curiosity led to early pioneering efforts, now legendary, that continue to contribute to both industry evolution and the supreme quality of award-winning, estate-bottled wines.

Left & Facing Page: David Bruce Winery's longstanding mission is to create the greatest pinot noir the world has ever tasted.
Photographs by M.J. Wickham

Mother Nature provides the palette of ingredients. First is the noble robe. It is that beautiful color that implies the abundant extraction that a great wine must have. "Color is the engine that pulls the pinot noir train," says David. Secondly comes a velvety texture, those wonderfully soft tannins that anoint the palate and coerce you to have another bite to eat—David Bruce Winery's pinot noir has that velvety texture from the first sip. Lastly, there is a distinct fruit-forwardness, a mixture of varietal fruit and spices that soothes the senses and proves beyond a doubt that heaven is real.

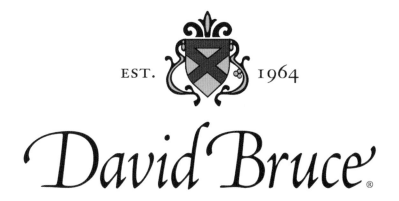

Wine & Fare

2005 Estate Chardonnay, Santa Cruz Mountains
Pair with delicate, light green dumplings like gnocchi verde and altico falcone.

2005 Estate Pinot Noir, Santa Cruz Mountains
Pair with lapin poêlé à la moutarde—rich and savory rabbit stew in mustard sauce with green peppercorns.

2007 Pinot Noir, Russian River Valley
Pair with herb-roasted leg of lamb rubbed with crushed garlic, salt, pepper and olive oil, sprinkled with marjoram, thyme and rosemary.

2007 Chardonnay, Russian River Valley
Pair with poulet marengo, chicken in wine with tomato sauce, topped with famous wild Burgundy ceps.

Tastings
Open to the public daily, year-round

Soquel Vineyards

Santa Cruz County

Nestled on a hillside amid the Santa Cruz Mountains lies picturesque Soquel Vineyards with sweeping Pacific vistas, a boutique winery where vintners passionately produce exceptional wines that are barrel-aged in artisan cooperage made from 200-year-old oak trees. It is this Old World, handcrafted heritage combined with modern winemaking expression that has made entrepreneurial founders Peter and Paul Bargetto, with fellow owner Jon Morgan, household names throughout the appellation. Third-generation winemakers, the Bargetto family has a long-established presence in the region; it was 1933 when the twins' grandfather John Bargetto founded the family's first winery and utilized choice grapes from select vineyards to make outstanding wine in the Italian tradition. Peter and Paul followed in their grandfather's footsteps, with a twist.

The adventurous trio of Peter, Paul and Jon began Soquel Vineyards in 1987 with the vision of creating nouveau-style wines that would capture the essence of estate grapes thriving on their newly acquired terroir. Just four miles from the rugged Monterey Bay coastline, Soquel Vineyards boasts an ideal climate and ancient soils that produce robust grapes for wines with vibrant color and elegance. Today the winemakers create 5,000 cases of award-winning, appellation-inspired pinot noir and nebbiolo from their estate vineyard, as well as classic cabernet sauvignon, merlot and zinfandel from select mountain vineyards. Above all, the environmentally conscious owners are passionately committed to farming organically. The limited-production winery has an intrinsic beauty, an Italianesque character that visitors find compelling. Soquel Vineyards borrowed its name from the indigenous Soquel Indian tribe that once inhabited a nearby town. Whatever its inspiration, Soquel Vineyards renders well balanced wines with a taste of cultural heritage in every bottle.

Top Left: The Soquel estate vineyard produced its first harvest in 2008, yielding a limited 350 cases of handcrafted pinot noir.

Middle Left: Old World craftsmanship is combined with modern winemaking, creating wines of distinction and style.

Bottom Left: The limited-production Soquel Vineyards winery is dedicated to rendering high-quality and well-balanced wines.

Facing Page: Guests always enjoy spectacular views from the boutique hilltop winery, which is perched on a ridgeline overlooking the majestic Monterey Bay.
Photographs by Maria Villano

Thomas Fogarty
Winery & Vineyard

Woodside

In the premier grape-growing region of the Santa Cruz Mountains AVA a passion for winemaking flourishes. Thomas Fogarty Winery & Vineyard has put down deep roots as the heart and soul of viticulture on the Pacific Coast Range. Its stunning property consists of 325 acres amid mountain glens, mudstone hilltops and windy enclaves on a 2,000-foot elevation—difficult conditions for farming—resulting in determined vineyard blocks that produce world-class fruit. Founded by internationally renowned Stanford cardiovascular surgeon and inventor Dr. Thomas Fogarty, the rugged piece of land was just one of the owner's fortuitous discoveries, where he eagerly planted his first vines in 1978. Prized chardonnay and pinot noir with small lots of merlot, cabernet sauvignon and cabernet franc thrive on six distinct estate vineyards today.

Along with inventing the lifesaving catheter in 1969, Dr. Fogarty's inspired journey is also about contributing to the health and enjoyment of those who desire character-filled Santa Cruz Mountains wines. Health of the vine and wellness of the body are two of the American vintner's commitments; he was intrigued by "The French Paradox," a study that identified the benefits of drinking red wine, unlocking the secret "fountain of youth" ingredient in grape skins. This valuable research supported the budding vintner's winemaking venture, and in 1981 he opened his winery doors. For more than three decades Dr. Fogarty has grown varietals that struggle in the chilly vineyards, ripening into the most intensely flavored fruit. These highly concentrated grapes yield limited-production Thomas Fogarty wines, all creatively handcrafted by head viticulturist-winemaker Michael Martella. Michael strives to capture sites, soils, and vines in every drop of exceptional wine—a heartfelt promise that the boutique winery keeps—so guests always experience a true reflection of the fruit.

Top Left: Showcasing spectacular Bay Area views, the winery Hill House is a popular venue for private events and weddings.
Photograph courtesy of Thomas Fogarty Winery & Vineyard

Middle & Bottom Left: Thomas Fogarty Winery's chardonnay lineup features fine single-vineyard designated estate chardonnays. Morning Coastal fog blankets San Francisco Bay, which plays a significant role in ripening the estate pinot noir and chardonnay fruit.
Middle Photograph by J. Pearlman Photography
Bottom Photograph by Michael Martella

Facing Page: The Thomas Fogarty estate winery offers a rare confluence of great vineyard sites and sweeping panoramas.
Photograph by Anne Krolczyk

Seguin Moreau Napa Cooperage, page 214

Bien Nacido Vineyards, page 206

Steinbeck Vineyards & Winery, page 218

Behind the Wines

Anne Thull Fine Art Designs

San Francisco

The beauty of the vineyard expressed through bronze sculpture epitomizes the talent and artistry of Anne Thull. Her design philosophy is to create timeless art pieces that are practical, yet possess a real wow factor. She honors her grandfather's vineyards in Naples, Italy, which cultivated fond childhood memories, such as her mother's cuttings from mature estate vines that were lovingly transplanted to the family home in Michigan. These grapevines inspired Anne's first lost-wax method bronze sculptures: the limited-edition, vineyard series light fixtures. This is but one idea behind Anne's museum-quality, sculptural lighting designs.

With heartfelt passion and flawless craftsmanship Anne has been designing and manufacturing "architectural art" including bespoke entry doors, cabinetry, fireplace surrounds, libraries and wine cellars; she creates "functional art" in custom light fixtures, unique furniture, built-ins, candle sleeves, LED flicker lamps and more. The designer also focuses on "fine art" creations that take form as original paintings, elegant sculpture and thematic wall murals. Each product is made to dramatize the architectural and structural design of home and work environments. Above all, she creates unique designs that are at once functional, but more than that, truly inspirational and timeless. Anne's high quality wood, bronze, metal, stone and art glass pieces are privately commissioned throughout the Bay Area, in wine country and internationally. Her gallery collection exhibits a sensitive artistic style. "Crafting fine wine and fine art are both aesthetic expressions. I work to elicit an emotional response," says Anne.

Top Right: *Standing in the Vineyard* lighted bronze sculptures are interpretations of old growth grapevines. Artistic options include interior or exterior patinas with custom variations.

Middle Right: *Old Growth Grapevine with Bird* and its companion sconce, *Old Growth Grapevine with Bird's Nest*, are from the Vineyard Series.

Bottom Right: The limited-edition *Standing in the Vineyard* lighted bronze grapevine sculpture features a weather-resistant patina.

Facing Page: *Standing in the Vineyard* is a limited-edition, lighted bronze sculpture of true-size old growth grapevines.
Photographs by Sasha Gulish

Bien Nacido Vineyards

Santa Maria Valley

Designated as one of the world's leading vineyards, Bien Nacido Vineyards has a family history of excellence as a California wine grape producer. The original enterprise was started in 1973 by Stephen TB Miller and Robert N. Miller IV in the heart of the Central Coast's respected Santa Maria Valley appellation; today, Stephen and his son Nicholas run the multifaceted business. Known for producing ultra-premium, cool-climate wine grapes, the five-generation farming family have been huge proponents of sustainable viticulture. As responsible stewards of the land, they are committed to offering highly customized farming services specific to the needs of their winemaking clientele throughout California. Ranch properties include Bien Nacido Vineyards, Solomon Hills Vineyards and French Camp Vineyards.

Since first planting their land with plants from UC Davis, the vineyards have expanded into an industry-recognized growth block producing low-yield, superior-quality fruit. "We start with the best plant material and, therefore, have the best quality production," says Nicholas. Early best practices included using steel-post trellising and drip irrigation systems—adopted across the industry today—on their two-tons-per-acre vineyard. The first to plant cool climate syrah in California, which is now farmed using biodynamic methods, the Millers also employ composting methods, solar panel gates and owl boxes for pest control. Vineyard manager Chris Hammell and viticulturist Greg Phelan work to stay true to the green philosophy—often exceeding sustainability standards—and together have achieved the important Sustainability in Practice™ certification for the whole vineyard operation.

Top Right: Spring bursts forth at French Camp Vineyards in Paso Robles.
Photograph by Kirk Irwin

Middle Right: Solomon Hills Vineyards thrives in the Santa Maria Valley.
Photograph by Kirk Irwin

Bottom Right: The hillside of Bien Nacido Vineyards showcases coveted soil.
Photograph by Chris Leshinsky

Facing Page: A morning fog cools Bien Nacido Vineyards in the Santa Maria Valley AVA.
Photograph by Adam Felde

The diverse growing region with its nutrient-rich terroir enjoys a unique phenomenon due to transverse mountains that extend to the Pacific; ridgelines act as a funnel by pulling in morning fog to maintain cool temperatures, then fog burns off in the afternoon allowing sunny, warm weather to do its work. Shining star varietals include chardonnay, pinot noir and cool-climate syrah; when ripened to perfection they are transformed into award-winning regional vintages. *Wine & Spirits Magazine* designated Bien Nacido as one of the world's best vineyards. The proprietors are proud of their "white glove" approach to custom farming, designing individual growing plans for each client. In addition to being a significant source of world-class grapes for some of the most illustrious vintners in California, the family's Central Coast Wines Services and Paso Robles Wine Services operations also provide custom winemaking partnerships, offering wine production, barrel and case good storage, bottling, lab analysis and assistance with compliance issues for more than 50 boutique wineries.

Interestingly, the Spanish phrase Bien Nacido means well born, but its colloquial translation means "born with a silver spoon." This name conveys that grapes harvested on the Millers' soil have been given every possible advantage. At Bien Nacido Vineyards, all decisions are made from this point of view to achieve superior quality fruit and maintain an unmatched reputation on the Central Coast.

Top Left: Block Z at Bien Nacido Vineyards extends into the vista.
Photograph by Adam Felde

Bottom Left: Stephen and Nicholas Miller have a rich history of premium winegrape growing and are advocates of sustainable farming.
Photographs by Chris Leshinsky

Facing Page Top: The dense fog rolling through a hillside block at Bien Nacido Vineyards is a daily phenomenon.
Photograph by Adam Felde

Facing Page Bottom Left: Central Coast Wine Services Winery in Santa Maria partners with area vintners.
Photograph by Kirk Irwin

Facing Page Bottom Right: Paso Robles Wine Services Winery in Paso Robles lends a hand to boutique wineries.
Photograph by Nicholas Miller

Chronic Cellars

Paso Robles

Chronic Cellars opened its doors in June 2008, but the seed of an idea was planted five years earlier when the two founder-brothers were relaxing with friends after a grape harvest. They were covered in juice, stained and tired when they had an epiphany. How about making wines to appeal to a young crowd so new wine drinkers would feel completely comfortable at tastings, even if they didn't know a thing about wine or the history of winemaking?

Josh and Jake Beckett were immersed in the wine country lifestyle as kids and grew up around the whole vintner culture through their family's business. It was only natural that they became passionate about the industry. Today making and selling great wine to call their own is a way of life, but their brand has an edgy personality. Josh and Jake are into motocross and extreme sports so there's a feeling of excitement at Chronic Cellars that no other winery establishment can live up to. The owners are far from stuffy. They hate stuffy. Chronic Cellars wines reflects this maverick mindset. A sketched skull and cross bones marks each label, almost inviting visitors to "pick your poison," as the old expression goes. The handcrafted wines are deliciously intoxicating. Sofa King Bueno, La Muñeca, Petite Sirah and El Perfecto are just some of the wonderful reds that Josh dreams up in his winemaking laboratory. Experimental and experiential sums up the tasting room atmosphere at Chronic Cellars, a place where guests can imbibe in the lively tasting room, sample new vintages and swap stories with friends and locals.

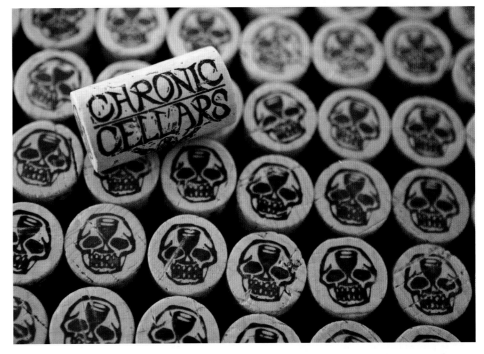

Top Right: Upbeat winemakers Josh and Jake Beckett enjoy a glass of Chronic and toast to long life.

Middle Right: The winery's infamous skull icon corks each bottle of wine.

Bottom Right: Chronic's late harvest zinfandel and Rhône-style white blend boast colorful folk art characters.

Facing Page: Chronic Cellars' tasting room architecture greets guests with an inviting yet edgy mystique.
Photographs by Josh Kimball

Rhone Rangers

Paso Robles

Call them rebels, mavericks or Wild West cowboys. Rhone Rangers has tremendous horsepower and was officially founded in 1997—originally formed by a dozen winemakers who wanted to produce something other than chardonnay and cabernet. California's wine evolution has been greatly influenced by this group of winemakers who share an affinity for growing France's revered Rhône Valley varietals and make incredible Rhône-style wines.

The organization's clever moniker is a play on words from the 1950s American radio and television series *The Lone Ranger*. Akin to the iconic masked character's heroic mission, Rhone Rangers is spreading the word about 22 grape varieties traditionally grown in France. The organization boasts 200 winery members, primarily from California's Central Coast, and extending to Napa, Sonoma and Mendocino Counties, Washington, Oregon and Idaho. For a wine to qualify as a Rhone Ranger wine, 75 percent of its contents must contain one or more of the 22 traditional Rhône grape varieties as approved by the French government for inclusion in the wines of the Côtes du Rhône. A few of the permitted grape varieties include best known syrah and viognier, up-and-coming mourvedre, grenache and roussanne, and the truly obscure but delicious counoise, bourboulenc and picpoul. "For me, the most exciting Rhone Ranger wines are blends of two, three, or even more of these grapes. Blending allows the winemaker to take advantage of their complementary characteristics, and results in wines that are easy to pair with many foods," says Cheryl Quist, Rhone Rangers executive director.

Top Right: Select wines crafted by Rhone Rangers' member wineries tempt the most sophisticated palate.

Middle & Bottom Right: Mourvèdre grapes impart rich, earthy character, syrah provides dark color with spicy notes, roussanne gives a lovely texture and grenache yields flavors of currants and black pepper.

Facing Page: Harvest at Tablas Creek Vineyard in Paso Robles is beautifully fruitful. Rhône varietals are widespread in the vineyards of California's Central Coast.
Photographs by Bob Dickey

Seguin Moreau Napa Cooperage

Napa

For a thousand years wine barrels were looked upon as just containers, a way to keep the wine from soaking into the ground. These fruits of the cooper's trade, however, were and are the image of wine—the romance of winemaking lies in the cellars where tall stacks of aged barrels hold quaffable charms. But not until fairly recent breakthroughs in technology did cooperages start to understand the effects that the wood has as wine swirls around in the belly of the barrel. Digging behind the romance, Seguin Moreau Napa Cooperage was the first to understand the interaction of wine and wood; and with a lot of strategy and a lot of science, the cooperage uses that romance to stoke the fire, as it were.

Seguin and Moreau began as separate cooperages, with Moreau founding in 1838 and Seguin in 1870. Located in the Charente region of France, near Bordeaux, the cooperages were in cognac territory, making barrels nearly exclusively for the cognac industry. In 1958, Remy Martin bought the two cooperages and combined them for its own purposes. Cognac had a great renaissance in the 1970s, but the demand for high-quality wine soon accelerated as well. Seeing a new opportunity, Seguin Moreau started producing barrels for wine, and an aggressive R&D campaign began. Very quickly it became evident to Seguin Moreau that wood types were of singular import.

Top Right: The cooperage, located in Napa, is the premier California creator of French oak barrels.

Middle Right: Fire and water are used to soften the wood, allowing the staves to be bent into shape.

Bottom Right: After shaping and toasting, barrels wait to be finished so that their aesthetic beauty equals the functional quality.

Facing Page: The first firing gives the barrel its shape. Upending the barrels, each end is hooped in turn, giving a blossomed-rose shape to the staves.
Photographs by M.J. Wickham

From this springboard, 25 years ago, Seguin Moreau became pioneers in wood science. A good barrel selection can offer structure and aromas of vastly varying degrees; the type of wood, the tightness of the grain and the level of toasting are each an important element in barrel selection. Part of the cooperage's technological prowess led to a method of wood seasoning called proactive maturation: the maturation of wood is monitored and controlled, based on meteorological data. Wood is carefully seasoned in Missouri and France, under the same principles in both places but with some differing details, according to oak species.

Because of the potentially infinite variety of barrels, almost every order that Seguin Moreau receives is custom made. To get to the exacting specifications of the winemaker the cooperage needed to have direct access on a daily basis; hence, Seguin Moreau became the first to produce French oak out of Napa for California wineries. The cooperage looks for understanding in their product, whether it is the effect on wine or on the earth—Seguin Moreau was the first cooperage to be certified by PEFC for its work with sustainable forest management. This reputation has resulted in heavy use—a dip into a Seguin Moreau barrel will draw out a glass of any of a number of the world's greatest wines.

Left: Coopering is a true combination of art and craft; years of training are the vital requisite for making great barrels.

Facing Page Top: The architecture of Seguin Moreau is specifically designed to integrate with the Napa Valley scenery.

Facing Page Bottom Left: The second firing creates the flavors that will work their way into the wines.

Facing Page Bottom Right: Seguin Moreau is the leader in French oak barrels, and the cooperage's crest can be found on the barrels of the most prestigious wines in the world.
Photographs by M.J. Wickham

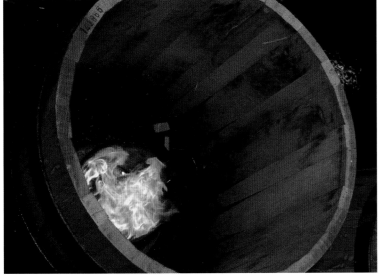

Steinbeck Vineyards & Winery

Paso Robles

The Steinbeck family has a rich history of farming on the Central Coast and an unending pioneering spirit dating back to the 1870s. Their remarkable property has been in the family since 1921, with grandfathers, fathers, daughters and sons cultivating agricultural crops to make a living off the land. Following in his great grandfather's grape-growing footsteps, Howie Steinbeck, with wife Bev, planted their first wine-grapes in 1982, supplying area wineries with premium, sustainably grown fruit. Today daughter and son-in-law Cindy and Tim Newkirk take the reins in leading an earnest mission to preserve and enhance their six-generation farm. The Steinbecks are honored to be stewards of their history and fertile soil; they celebrate the past, cherish today and work toward a successful future.

This limited-production boutique winery judiciously creates up to 3,000 cases of estate-grown wines annually, hand selecting blocks from its 500-acre vineyard. Four individual varietals—cabernet sauvignon, petite syrah, zinfandel and viognier—have been chosen from their 13 varietals grown. These are artfully combined to create the Steinbeck's proprietary red blend. Indeed, the winemaking prowess of award-winning vintner Steven Glossner makes the Steinbeck wines noteworthy. Steven encourages the ripe fruit to come forward, and then he finishes the wines with a pure velvet feel. Steinbeck Vineyards & Winery possesses a rustic elegance offering visitors an enriching experience with tastings and friendly Jeep tours, a fabulous way to see the prized vineyards and gather insight into the Steinbeck's heritage.

Top Right: Three generations all work together, building a legacy.

Middle Right: Expressing the Steinbeck's commitment to the future, this elegant wine portfolio speaks volumes about the family's passion.

Bottom Right: A 1958 Willy's Jeep nicknamed "WineYard Willy," transports visitors on educational adventures through the expansive vineyards.

Facing Page: Steinbeck Vineyards provides an enriching lifestyle for the family, premium fruit for local wineries and fun for guests.
Photographs by Richard Baker

Spectacular Wineries of California's Central Coast

California's Central Coast Team

Vice President, Regional Publisher: Carla Bowers

Vice President, Regional Publisher: Kathryn Newell

Graphic Designer: Ashley DuPree

Editor: Anita M. Kasmar

Production Coordinator: Drea Williams

Headquarters Team

Publisher: Brian G. Carabet

Publisher: John A. Shand

Executive Vice President: Phil Reavis

Director of Development & Design: Beth Benton Buckley

Publication & Circulation Manager: Lauren B. Castelli

Senior Graphic Designer: Emily A. Kattan

Graphic Designer: Kendall Muellner

Managing Editor: Rosalie Z. Wilson

Editor: Michael McConnell

Editor: Jennifer Neslon

Editor: Sarah Tangney

Editor: Lindsey Wilson

Managing Production Coordinator: Kristy Randall

Production Coordinator: Maylin Medina

Traffic Coordinator: Brandi Breaux

Administrative Manager: Carol Kendall

Administrative Assistant: Beverly Smith

Client Support Coordinator: Amanda Mathers

PANACHE PARTNERS, LLC

CORPORATE HEADQUARTERS

1424 Gables Court

Plano, TX 75075

469.246.6060

www.panache.com

www.panachewine.com

Talbott Vineyards, page 144

THE PANACHE COLLECTION

CREATING SPECTACULAR PUBLICATIONS FOR DISCERNING READERS

Dream Homes Series
An Exclusive Showcase of the Finest Architects, Designers and Builders

Carolinas
Chicago
Coastal California
Colorado
Deserts
Florida
Georgia
Los Angeles
Metro New York
Michigan
Minnesota
New England
New Jersey

Northern California
Ohio & Pennsylvania
Pacific Northwest
Philadelphia
South Florida
Southwest
Tennessee
Texas
Washington, D.C.

Spectacular Homes Series
An Exclusive Showcase of the Finest Interior Designers

California
Carolinas
Chicago
Colorado
Florida
Georgia
Heartland
London
Michigan
Minnesota
New England

New York
Ohio & Pennsylvania
Pacific Northwest
Philadelphia
South Florida
Southwest
Tennessee
Texas
Toronto
Washington, D.C.
Western Canada

Perspectives on Design Series
Design Philosophies Expressed by Leading Professionals

California
Carolinas
Chicago
Colorado
Florida
Georgia

Great Lakes
Minnesota
New England
Pacific Northwest
Southwest

Art of Celebration Series
The Making of a Gala

Chicago
Georgia
Midwest
New York
Philadelphia
South Florida
Southern California
Southwest
Texas
Washington, D.C.
Wine Country

Spectacular Wineries Series
A Captivating Tour of Established, Estate and Boutique Wineries

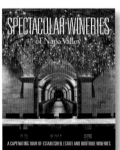

California's Central Coast
Napa Valley
New York
Sonoma County

Specialty Titles
The Finest in Unique Luxury Lifestyle Publications

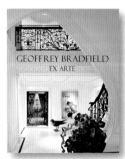

Cloth and Culture: Couture Creations of Ruth E. Funk
Distinguished Inns of North America
Extraordinary Homes California
Geoffrey Bradfield Ex Arte
Into the Earth: A Wine Cave Renaissance
Spectacular Golf of Colorado
Spectacular Golf of Texas
Spectacular Hotels
Spectacular Restaurants of Texas
Visions of Design

City by Design Series
An Architectural Perspective

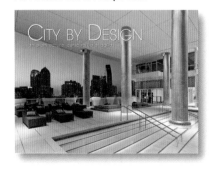

Atlanta
Charlotte
Chicago
Dallas
Denver
Orlando
Phoenix
San Francisco
Texas

PanacheWine.com
Where Wine Industry Experts Gather, Share and Inspire

PanacheWine.com overflows with beautiful photographs, tempting pairings and interesting articles by prominent winery proprietors and award-winning winemakers from California to New York. A gallery of vineyard-inspired photographs and a library of articles are among the comprehensive site's offerings.

Panache Partners, LLC • 1424 Gables Court • Plano, Texas 75075 • 469.246.6060 • www.panache.com

Conway Family Wines, *Photograph by Ian Shive*